THE PATH OF THE YOUNG MILLIONAIRE

The Blueprint to Wealth At a Young Age

Outsmart The Elite Financial System, Even When you Are Starting From Nothing

MICHAEL WOODS

FREE GIFT JUST FOR YOU!

Our comprehensive career guide will help you find a fulfilling career path that aligns with your desired lifestyle. Discover a wealth of diverse job options, practical business startup advice, unique and exciting business ideas, as well as valuable college degrees that are worth the investment.

Download NOW for exclusive access to these insights

Or go to http://michaelwoodslife.com

INTRODUCTION:

The way the world works is not as it is being presented. Most people are oblivious to how money and wealth building works. Your financial destiny is not dictated by your starting point, it is dictated by what you know, who you know, your decisions, and actions, and all of this is under your control.

This book is designed to make aware of the world around you, empower you to navigate the established systems and carve your path to wealth, working within and around these systems, starting from where you are right now. This book is for the ambitious, the dreamers, the knowledge seekers, and those who want something better for themselves. You will gain insight into how the world's wealth and power structures operate, understand your place within these structures, and learn how to navigate through them to find prosperity of your own. We delve deep into the societal, economic, and personal dynamics that govern our lives, offering a comprehensive understanding of the world in its entirety—the flawed systems that perpetuate wealth concentration at the top, the opportunities masked by the status quo, and the multitude of paths you can take towards financial independence.

We live in a world where most of the wealth is concentrated in the hands of a few while the rest of us are in a continuous cycle of paycheck-to-paycheck, struggling with money. There is a way out and I am going to show you the way.

We're going to challenge the status quo, push thru the financial systems that govern our lives, and reveal what is needed to escape a system that is designed to keep you stationary. You will find this knowledge, insights, and information accessible and applicable to your life, because the teachings here are universal, offering anyone the foundation they need to elevate their situation, generate more income, better understand the world's dynamics, pursue worthwhile endeavors, realize the opportunities that abound, and see the world with greater clarity.

This book acknowledges the uniqueness of each individual's journey towards financial independence. Everyone comes from different circumstances, harbors different interests, and possesses unique personalities. There are a lot of different paths to the good life, and escapes out of the system. Remember, the path to financial freedom is as unique as the individual walking it.

As you embark on this enlightening journey with us, I encourage you to navigate through this book at your own pace, the knowledge presented here will help you for the rest of your life, so take your own time to absorb the wealth of knowledge, insights, and strategies shared within these pages. Have these as one of your main manuals to transform your entire outlook on wealth, power, and success. Each chapter will build upon each other.

Do not overlook the first chapter where we cover the dynamics of the world's financial systems. We show you what you're up against which will be essential to find your way to prosperity. It's time to bring more light and clarity into your life and gain the hope you need to head where you want to go.

TABLE OF CONTENTS

CHAPTER 1:

Working Within The Established Financial System

Within the System: Understanding How the World Operates

We live in a complex world, where it takes a lifetime to understand how it works. I am going to do my best to give you an overview of the type of world we live in.

I want to focus in this section on the financial aspects of life. Most people around the world, even in developed countries like the US, the UK, Australia, etc, are trapped in what I like to call the "Financial Matrix" or just "The System," meaning most of us do NOT have the power to live our lives freely however we want. Most people are in a loop of going to work just to end up in the same place week after week, month after month, and unfortunately, year after year, living paycheck to paycheck. In most countries in the world the masses are living this way. There are a lot of people with money, of course, but it's safe to say that the masses are living paycheck to paycheck, and they do not have the financial stability they would like, often finding themselves constrained by the limitations of their earnings.

> *We work 8 hours to enjoy 4*
> *We work all year to enjoy only 2 weeks*
> *We work for most of our lives to retire*
> *in our old age*
> *There is something terribly wrong*
> *with this system*

If you are in this "financial matrix," you will find yourself in a constant struggle to balance income with expenses, where your job is often barely or even worse, not even enough to cover everyday expenses, saving is almost impossible, let alone having enough money to do what you want to do in life, like travel and more leisure time. So most people find themselves in this cycle until they die; most people never get out of it. Wishing they did.

This "Financial Matrix" encapsulates not just a cycle of economic dependency but a systematic structure that defines our choices, opportunities, our lifestyles, and ultimately, our freedom. If you are inside of a system, you will flow within the system. So being within its structure, means that we will flow with it and fall into the averages. And how are average people?

Multiple studies like the Federal Reserve's Report on the Economic Well-Being of U.S. Households and the U.S.

Bureau of Labor Statistics (BLS) will support that most people:

- Cannot afford a $500 emergency: This shows how vulnerable most people are to rainy days.

- Living Paycheck to Paycheck: Meaning after paying their main bills, (Housing, transportation and food) they have little to nothing until the next time they get paid.

- Burdened by Debt: So many people are with unsustainable amounts of debt across various forms, such as credit card debt, student loans, auto loans, and mortgages.

- With little to no savings or investments: Most people do not have anything saved and own assets or are well-suited for retirement. Meaning they will struggle badly in their old years.

- Lack of Financial Literacy: So many people do not understand money and have no comprehension skills about how the world works. They are passing through time, reacting to life.

And that is just scratching the surface.

The roots of these issues often trace back to systemic problems at the top of our institutions. Since these are flawed, those problems trickle down and affect everyone. Hera are some of the causes:

- Concentration of wealth and power among the global elite
- Lobbying by special interest groups to shape economic policies
- Monopolistic practices in banking and finance
- Media manipulation and control over public perception
- Political corruption and lack of accountability
- Influence of corporate money in politics
- Predatory investment in vulnerable economies
- Disinformation campaigns to discredit economic reforms
- Undermining public education to maintain class divisions
- Financing and profiting from military conflicts
- Lack of financial literacy programs
- Economic policies favoring the wealthy

And all the above cause the following problems:

- High cost of living
- Stagnant wages
- Inadequate social safety nets
- Job market volatility
- Unsustainable debt levels
- Inequality in wealth distribution
- Limited access to affordable healthcare

- Expensive higher education and student loans
- Inflation outpacing income growth
- Insufficient retirement planning and resources

So, if we would have better systems in place, it would be a lot easier for the masses to find prosperity, while we humans have achieved a lot over the last 100 years and in many ways the world is doing a lot better, we still have a long way to go in ensuring systems that work for most people and not just a few.

The good news is that there is a lot we can do to escape this; you have 100 percent control over what you do. So, if you understand a few concepts and learn to navigate through it, you can get out. The system doesn't make it easy for us, but we often make it even worse for ourselves. If we were working in our own favor, we could typically overcome everything else that is working against us to build wealth. The situation is hard in the first place, don't have your habits make your situation worse

And most people are not that greedy. Research and surveys often show that happiness levels would significantly increase if individuals had just a bit more leisure time and a slightly larger amount in their bank accounts. With just a bit more money, most people would be a lot happier.

The Elite Financial System: Wealth Concentration at the Top Levels:

You need to have a bit more insight to know what you are fighting against. We are getting just a bit deeper and then get into how you can get out of this system.

We need to be honest about one aspect:

If you are not born inside the circle of influence, you're outside of it.

It's a club and you're not in it.

Why is it so hard to get out of poverty, even more so to become financially stable, let alone build wealth? Well, it lies in the way societies organize their economies, distribute resources, and make policy decisions. First, I am going to tell you something that you may not know:

> *Mass poverty is NOT caused by a lack of resources but by exclusionary systems. Globally, there is enough wealth and resources to provide for the basic needs of all people, but the way in which these resources are allocated and controlled often leads to disparities and inequalities.*

Without getting too political because this is not a political book, there is an argument to be made that we actually live in a Plutocracy. The term "plutocracy" itself stems from the Greek words "ploutos" (wealth) and "kratos" (power or rule), describing a situation where wealth equals power. We live in a world...

- Of the wealthy
- By the wealthy
- For the wealthy

In a plutocratic system, the ultra-wealthy/world elites, have significant control over the governance and decision-making processes that influence the way we live within the system. This is a problem because often results in policies and practices that favor the interest of the most powerful and well-connected at the expense of everyone else. You can see this form of governance in various political systems, including democracies, where financial power influences political decisions also known as (special interests).

In such systems, the disparity between the rich and the poor is a matter of income, political influence, and access to resources. The primary issue in a plutocracy system is the profound economic inequality it perpetuates. Wealth concentration in the hands of a few creates vast economic inequality, making upward mobility for the masses more challenging, perpetuating a cycle of poverty. A lot of people think that these problems are coming from a lack of technicality, but it is more by design. The lack of these fundamental resources creates barriers that makes it a lot harder for people at the bottom to improve their economic situations while at the same time easy for the elite to maintain the status quo of wealth concentration at the top.

So we live in a system where is easy for the rich and powerful to thrive but very hard for the poor to get out.

<u>Let's be honest here:</u>

> ***The elites and their special interests influence world governments to maintain the status quo that favors them at the expense of everyone else.***

So we live basically in a "Socialism for the rich, capitalism for everyone else" type of system and this is what you are fighting against. You have to get out of a system that is designed to keep the privileges of a few, while the majority bear the costs.

Why do I say "Socialism for the rich"? Well, the wealthy and powerful enjoy all the benefits of government support and protection, akin to socialist ideals, while the poor face the brutalities of unforgiving market competition, as seen in pure capitalist systems. So, while the ultra-rich/elites get richer with the help of subsidies, bailouts, incentives, and tax cuts, the poor struggle to compete in an economic landscape where everybody is on their own. This is the reason why is harder for you than it should be to get out of poverty. You do not have this unfair advantage. If we had better systems in place that are more fair and they were designed to help people get out of poverty, it would be a lot easier for the masses to find prosperity. I am not denying there is a component of personal responsibility, of course there is, but the system does not make it easy for you, even if you are a hard worker, you can still be stuck in a loop of poverty. So it is a lot harder than it should be.

Don't think this is something new, since the beginning of time, the world has always had a few elites that have most of the control over how most people live their lives. This has always been the case. When I say "The system" I do not refer to one formal entity but rather a network of major financial institutions, governments, ultra-wealthy individuals, and powerful corporations that wield significant influence over not only the economy of one country but globally as well. So, they are key players with immense wealth and power structuring the system we all live in, I'll give you a few examples:

- Multinational Corporations
- Government Institutions (FBI, CIA, NSA)
- Big banks/ Wall St / Federal Reserve / IMF
- The Military Industrial Complex / Military Contractors
- Mainstream Media / Corporate Media
- Elite Families
- Organized Crime (The Mafia)
- Non-Profit Organizations.

There is more; these actors are on the main list.

That list constitutes what many people like to call *"The Blob"* *"The Deep State,"* or *"The Establishment,"* which refers to the top leadership in global politics and the broader power structures and elites in society. The concentration of wealth and power in the hands of the few that dictates the economic realities for the many

It is important to note that these institutions and groups are not necessarily always working explicitly together. However, they have undeniable shared interests, such as the accumulation of capital and power, among others and a significant impact on the economy and the broader societal context in which the masses live. Their actions directly impact economic policies, social norms, and the overall direction of both national and global developments.

Let me give you a perspective, for you to take dimension of what I am talking about. According to the Credit Suisse Global Wealth Report 2022, the top 1% of the world's wealthiest people owned about 45.6% of the world's wealth. Meaning only a few thousands of people hold half of the world's wealth, keep in mind that the world has over 7 billion people. This statistic highlights the significant disparity in wealth distribution not only by country but on a global scale. I know you may think this is unfair and it is, but you must accept reality for what it is and that is the world we live in for what it is.

Let's put as an example The United States, the richest, most powerful country in the world, the situation is not a lot better. The Federal Reserve's Distributional Financial Accounts indicate that as of the end of 2022, the top 1% of Americans by wealth owned approximately 32% of all household wealth in the U.S. So, as you see we live in a world where most of the wealth is concentrated at the top and the system that they create keeps most of the money flowing in one direction up and round, between them, (Up and around). This slows down progress.

Of course, all of this varies a lot by country, some have it better than others and in countries with more severe systemic issues, poverty manifests through extreme deprivation and lack of basic necessities, but even in nations considered to be part of the "First World" or economically advanced, developed countries a substantial portion of the population still lives paycheck to paycheck. So generally, the principle remains the same, but of course, depending on how bad the system is you will see how poverty is expressed. Understanding this will help you comprehend the workings of the global economy and the distribution of economic power and resources.

I am not giving you this news to discourage you; it is still a lot easier to achieve wealth now than it was 20 or 50 years ago. I am telling you this for you to understand the system you find yourself in and why you are somewhat on your own to make things happen, because the government, unfortunately, will not help you. When was the last time your government implemented a policy that benefited you personally? It is rare when it happens. Unfortunately, for the most part, the system leaves you to figure it out, and you must learn to navigate it. This is the game you are playing, and it is probably a bit of a red pill you have to swallow.

The good news is that the system still allows for the ones who push hard enough the ability to get out, you must learn to operate within its constraints while simultaneously seeking ways to create your own financial independence. So it is not impenetrable or impossible, it is just hard. The digital age has democratized access to information and financial tools, providing unprecedented opportunities for wealth creation. There are a lot more people finding wealth faster and easier now than during most of history, and that is great news for you.

So, this is a game, play it, and enjoy the ride. If you play the game smartly, using the tools available to you in this modern age. You cannot just survive within the system but to thrive despite of it.

I am going to provide you a quote from John McAfee on, societal power dynamics and awareness:

The 1% controls the world
About 4% are instruments to uphold the existing order
90% of people are sleep
5% of people know it and try to wake up the other 90%

The top 1% diligently works to ensure that the 5% who are awake fail in waking up the remaining 90%.

The Paycheck-to-Paycheck Loop We're All in

After talking about all of this we need to talk about you, since you probably were not born with wealth and inside of this circle of influence.

According to the LendingClub Corporation and PYMNTS Research, As of 2023, a significant portion of the U.S. population was living paycheck to paycheck. In June 2023, it was reported that 61% of U.S. consumers found themselves in this situation. Given the statistics, you are probably in this situation.

I probably do not have to explain to you how this much because you know it very well:

You rely entirely on each paycheck to cover living expenses, with little to no extra money for anything else other than your bills, and sometimes you cannot even cover all of your bills. This mode of living, common among a wide range of income levels, is characterized by a continual reliance on the next paycheck to meet current financial obligations. People in this situation find it challenging to set aside funds for savings, investments, side projects, or emergency expenses, let alone build wealth and having enough.

Let's be honest about something, not having money sucks, it really sucks, it makes life harder in every aspect, it makes your problems harder to solve, your lifestyle, not the one you would like to have and it limits you in everything you want to do. You often feel that having even just a little bit of extra money would help solve some if not most of your problems. The emotional and psychological toll of constant financial stress on people is profound. Being always stressed about money affects your overall well-being and outlook on life. Unfortunately, most people live this way.

<u>So there are three ways to look at this:</u>

You have a spending problem: (You make good money but you spend too much)

You have an income problem: (You don't spend that much, but you don't make much either)

Worse yet. You have both: (You don't make that much money and you spend a lot of money, this is what gets you into debt)

You have to look at yourself and see where you are with this, do you have an income problem, a spending problem, or both?

Because with different income, you can have the opposite problem, meaning you can be in a situation where even though your income may not be that high since your expenses are low, you can be in a better financial position than someone who is making a lot more money than you but their expenses are very high.

**Example:**

Scenario 1: Modest Income, Low Stress

Michael earns $45,000 a year and lives simply in a cost-effective area. He rents an affordable apartment, drives a reliable older car, and he mostly cooks at home, he does not buy a lot of stuff and lives moderately . This allows him to have more money to spend in other ventures and pursue a desired lifestyle.

Scenario 2: High Income, High Stress

Alex makes $150,000 annually but lives in an expensive city. His income is quickly absorbed by a luxury apartment, a new car lease, and a lifestyle filled with high-end dining and fashion to keep up with social circles and also, he loves to buy unnecessary stuff.

Despite earning a lot less, Michael is less financially stressed than Alex. I do this to show you that high earners also can live paycheck to paycheck, and they do.

How do you get out of this situation? I am going to cover this next.

The Transactional Nature of Money: A New Look at Money Acquisition

To be able to leave this system you need a different perspective on money.

We all heard the term "Making money" but is "making" the correct word when we acquire or we are taking it from someone else? You are probably not the Federal Reserve or the Central Bank so you don't "Make Money". The reality is the following: You "take" money from something or someone when you acquire it.

This applies to everything you can think of:

- Employee to Employer:

Example: An employee works for a company and receives a salary.

Transaction: Money moves from the employer (company) to the employee in exchange for their labor and skills.

- Customer to Business (Product Purchase):

Example: A customer buys a smartphone from an electronics store.
Transaction: Money moves from the customer to the business in exchange for the smartphone.

- Service Provider to Client:

Example: A freelance graphic designer creates a logo for a client.
Transaction: Money moves from the client to the service provider (freelancer) in exchange for the design services.

- Tenant to Landlord:

Example: A tenant pays rent to live in an apartment.
Transaction: Money moves from the tenant to the landlord in exchange for housing.

- Bank Loan to Borrower:

Example: A person takes out a mortgage loan from a bank to buy a house.
Transaction: Money moves from the bank to the borrower, who then pays the seller of the house. The borrower will repay the bank over time, with interest.

- Consumer to Restaurant:

Example: A family dines at a restaurant and pays for their meal.
Transaction: Money moves from the consumers (family) to the restaurant in exchange for food and service.

I can go on and on..

This transactional perspective emphasizes that money in an economy is continuously changing hands, fueling the activities and exchanges that keep the economy functional. In essence, money is not created out of thin air; at least not between people. It is transferred from one entity to another in exchange for something of value. This transactional nature of money is fundamental to understanding how economies operate.

This concept leads to an important realization: When we talk about **making** money, we are essentially talking about **'taking'** or receiving money from someone else in exchange for something. So money doesn't 'grow' – It 'moves'. You don't create it, you <u>EARN</u> it through transactions that move money from one entity to you.

> *"The act of making money is more about earning it through participation in transactions that facilitate this movement of funds from one party to you"*

This could be in the form of goods, services, or labor. The perceived value of what you offer determines how much others are willing to pay in exchange for it.

If you are able to understand and internalize this transactional nature of money, it can be a game-changer in how you approach life and your finances and ideas will start flowing to your mind about the different ways you can make *(Take)* money. This realization is powerful because it shifts the focus from the vague concept of 'making money' to the more tangible and actionable idea of 'creating value'.

When you start to see money as medium that moves in exchange for value, you start to realize different possibilities for increasing your income. For example, if you're an employee, you might think about enhancing your skills, taking on additional responsibilities to increase your value to your employer, changing roles where you can increase your contribution, or getting another job where the value you provide is more, so you can make more. As a business owner, you could focus on improving the quality of your products or services to attract more customers or increasing the amount of people that you are providing your value to. As an aspiring entrepreneur, you can come up with ideas that fulfill a need or solve a problem in the market which will create value for potential customers. This way of seeing money will lead to innovative approaches to income generation. You want to explore side hustles that align with your skills and interests, offering services or products that cater to a niche market, (A group of people).

Remember:

- Money is circulating all the time, its all around us.
- Money doesn't just appear; it moves in response to the value provided.
- Money is not made, it is taken.

Understanding this is crucial in your journey to financial independence.

What It Takes To Liberate Yourself From The Financial Matrix

Much of your approach to the world depends on your mindset, your experiences, and who you are as a whole which will translate into how you live day by day. Because you need to shift what you are doing day by day to allow progress to come into flow with your life.

You need to behave and act in a certain way for the next 5-10 years, What you do over the next years of your life is going to dictate if you are going to live a life or financial abundance or not. I want you to know something:

> *"You don't see the world as it is, you see it as you are"*

You are probably tired of seeing people that are not that much smarter than you, not much more skilled than you, yet they are able to make a lot more money than you because they know a few things that you don't, or they have done a few things that you did not or they know some people that you don't. The things I am going to cover next are going to take a bit of time for the idea to sink in/ "click" with you, but more importantly, it is going to take even more time for you to do something about it, but learning these things, will plant a seed of awareness in your mind that can change the course of your life.

Insight # 1: You Need A New Perspective on Time And Money

Time is given to you, we all have a limited amount of heartbeats and time on this earth. You need to learn to use most of it and not waste it with unproductive activities. You need to learn how to use time, (Day by day week by week, month by month, year by year) as the vehicle for you to achieve your financial goals and personal aspirations. Time is the most valuable resource you have, and unlike money, it cannot be earned back. You can lose $1000 now and make it back in the future. But you cannot be 25 years old now and be 25 years old again in the future.

Once time it's gone, **IT IS GONE.**

So since time is given to you, it needs to be used for good and waste as little as possible doing unproductive/ unfulfilling activities. (Videogames, scrolling down social media, Streaming services, etc) You have to optimize your time in a way that aligns with your long-term goals and act accordingly every day. Also, it's not just about how many hours you work, but how effectively you use those hours. Successful entrepreneurs understand this. They prioritize tasks that maximize their time's value, focusing on activities that offer the greatest returns, both financially and personally. So, time is money.

Regarding money, you must shift your perspective from seeing it merely as a means to an end. The intrinsic value of life is beyond pieces of papers or numbers on a screen. ***Money is a a tool, that's it.***

Money is merely a tool you use for your advantage for things such as creating opportunities, achieving stability and leveraging resources, including the time and skills of others, keep that in mind. That is why to make money you need to spend money, whether you realize it or not, have a business or not. You are spending money to make it, I'll give you some examples: To get a job you probably had to spend some money on a drug test, clothing to look good for the interview, gas for your car, etc. Same to keep your job. You have to spend on your lunch, your monthly gas expenses, your insurance, etc. Whether you realize it or not, you always have money working for you. When you go out to a restaurant, you use your money to have the server come to serve you, you have chefs cook food for you. Our daily lives are filled with examples of money working for us. When we buy groceries, we're essentially paying for the convenience and labor of others who have farmed, transported, and packaged these goods. When we pay for utilities like electricity and water, we're using our money to ensure a continuous supply of these essential services. Now that you probably understand this concept: I am going to teach you how to get your money to work for you to generate more money: Shift your mindset from going from "Money focused" to "Lifestyle focused.". Because the mere position of money has not value, only the purpose for which it is used.

What I am trying to say that money is a tool **<u>NOT THE GOAL.</u>**

This approach leads to being less stressed about the numbers on a screen on your bank account or the amount of paper that you have in your wallet and more focused on the more tangible things of life that you feel day by day. That's what really matters in your life (Your health, your relationships, your stability, and your progress towards your long-term goals.). All of this can help you live life in a more fulfilling way. Now, to clarify: we are not saying that money isn't important, of course, it is. I am just trying to make you understand this because detaching yourself from the obsession with just accumulating money makes it easier to get more of it (surprisingly).

Like I said before, the value of money IS NOT in its mere possession, the value of money is in its utilization and the purposes it serves for you, since you can use it to satisfy your basic needs, obtain wants or needs, you can also use it to facilitate your path to wealth. This shift in mindset will help you getting out of a system that is designed to keep you poor. (The financial Matrix).

Insight # 2 You Need to Understand That Things Take Time:

We live in a world of social media and a world of instant gratification where it seems like everyone has it so well and wealth and money can come fast. I am sorry to pop your bubble, but this is just not the case. Just because you see it on social media often, doesn't mean that it is common for people to become millionaires quickly. The world doesn't work that way, Does it happen for some people? Sure, is it the norm? Absolutely not.

Building wealth takes time, and more so when you are starting from nothing. You need to know right now that if you find yourself in an unfavorable situation when it comes to money, it may take you 1-3 years at least just to improve your situation and be stable. (Assuming you are doing most things right), building wealth will take longer. Significant achievements rarely happen overnight, and when and if they do happen, they are typically short-lived. You want to build something that is going to stay with you in the long run and these things are the result of consistent effort, learning, and adaptation over time. The journey of building wealth or achieving personal goals is not a sprint but a marathon. You need to erase and rewire your brain from TikTok and social media for quick results and understand that the journey will take longer than you think.

Think about this: What can you do or build in 1 month that will pay you or stay with you for the next 10 years? Can you think of something? Because I can't. Big things that will stay for the long haul take years to build, and a lot more than just one month. Also, you want to know something? it is better if you do it that way!

Fast money comes with small problems, you probably heard that saying before. Meaning that, sometimes, fast money that is made through means that are either legally questionable or outright illegal can lead to a host of legal problems that could take a long time to resolve if you can resolve them at all. Especially if you live in first-world countries with strong institutions and legal systems like the United States, Canada, The UK, etc. "quick wealth", (Which is rare, it is not as common as social media portrays it) typically comes from volatile sources like gambling, stock market speculation, selling drugs, short-term business success, scamming, or other related activities. These are not sustainable ventures in the long run, IF they work, they only work for you at the moment and maybe over the next few months of your life. This creates a false sense of security, leading to problems when the money stops flowing as freely. Also, you need to keep in mind that this type of money it is typically "Active Income", meaning you have to keep doing what you are doing to keep the flow IF you can keep it, it is not passive at all. Also keep in mind that quick wealth like this especially when it's unexpected or comes without the gradual experience of managing money, leads to poor financial decisions and overspending since these individuals do not have the skills or experience to manage a lot of money wisely, ending up with long-term financial difficulties, debt and bankruptcy (On top of possible legal issues). There are plenty of examples of this. You want to stay away from this. Put your focus on building things, whether is a career or a business that is going to stay with you over the next 5-10 years minimum.

We live in one of the best times to do this because achieving wealth is easier than ever before and you can do it faster than ever before. There are ways to 'speed up' the process without bypassing it since there are so many different businesses and career paths you could take that if you give it 1-3 years of your life it can leave you in a great financial situation and set you up, maybe for the rest of your life, because you will keep improving and advancing once you are at a certain point. One key approach to 'speeding up' the process of wealth accumulation is through leveraging the power of technology and the internet. In today's digital age, there are countless opportunities to create businesses or work in careers that were not possible just 15 years ago. E-commerce, digital marketing, online businesses and content creation are just a few examples of areas where diligent work over a few years can yield significant financial rewards. These fields often have lower barriers to entry and offer the potential for scalable income, meaning your earnings can grow disproportionately to the amount of time you invest. We will be expanding on this later in the book.

Insight # 3: There are two main ways for you to achieve financial independence: You can **EARN** your way there, or you can **OWE** your way there.

OWNING You Way There:

When I say you can owe your way to financial wealth, I mean leveraging investments or assets that can generate income, whether passive or active that can appreciate significantly over time, potentially leading to a rapid accumulation of wealth. You may probably think you have nothing you can leverage right now, but that's where the journey begins. You can start small and gradually building your system, which it will take you a few years to do.

Real estate, for example, has historically been a reliable way to build wealth. Even if you can't afford to buy a property outright, you can still get a home with a downpayment and good credit. There are ways to get involved in real estate investing, such as real estate investment trusts (REITs), crowdfunding platforms, or even partnering with others on a property investment. The idea is to put your money into assets that are likely to appreciate over time, providing you with a return on your investment.

EARNING Your Way There:

Earning your way to financial independence revolves around maximizing and prioritizing INCOME rather than ownership. That can be done through employment, professional activities, or a business you can start growing. This path is about leveraging your skills, put your talents to work and generate a steady and increasing flow of income thru endeavors. For most people this begins with a traditional job while strategically transitioning into some career. Your purpose is to increase your value to the world. The more you contribute to the world and adapt to your market, the higher your salary will be.

To simplify and clarify:

The focus of **Owning** is on investing in assets. The focus of **earning** is on maximizing your income through traditional employment or professional activities.

The path to ownership is less about starting your own business and more about investing in existing assets that can grow independently of your day-to-day efforts. The path of earning is more about increasing your income through work, which can include running your own business, focusing on a specific career, making more money at your job, etc. Both paths have different strategies and focus areas for achieving financial independence.

The best strategy is to do both, but starting with the side of earning first (Because you need money to make money). You want to focus on increasing your income through a job, career, or business. Then, once you start to build wealth, you can start to invest in assets.

I have created a six-step process for you to achieve financial liberation. Using this method, you can gain financial independence in 3-5 years.

Step 1: You need a Stable Income (1-6 Months)

If you are in a position where you live with your parents and they pay all of your bills, sure, you can focus on starting something without a job. But if you don't, you need to put your ego to the side and get a job. Period. You cannot just be working on a new business with little or no experience and no money and expect to start generating income just like that. You need a secure and stable job that will support you while you build something. Most people have bills to pay and income thru new endeavors do not come right away. An income will help you cover basic living expenses and allow you to explore additional ventures more freely. Especially in the initial stages where everything is unknown, you need this stability; it is crucial and also acts as a buffer against the risks associated with entrepreneurial endeavors or investments. Do not feel the rush to be a full-time entrepreneur overnight. For most people, it is not going to happen. The process of finding a good-paying job where you are comfortable and stable can vary, but it can be done in under six months. So if you are not making a lot of money with your job now, work on getting another one where you can make more. If you income is good, work on lowering your expenses as much as you can. You want to be in a position where you are somehow financially stable.

Step 2: Identifying And Starting a Side Venture (6 months-1 year)

While you are working, you need to decide what are you going to pursue.

- Will it be a career?
- Will it be a college degree?
- Will it be entrepreneurship?

This will depend on your own personal interests and skills. You may decide to start a business, go to an apprenticeship, drive a truck, or go to college, whatever it is that aligns with your goals. Choosing the right side venture is a crucial step in escaping the unwanted financial situation you find yourself in.

It needs to be sustainable. You need to stop the "quick buck" mentality. That mentality takes you to always try new things that only last a few months, not seeing results and moving to the next thing, and start all over again when you don't see quick results. If you have a hobby that can be monetized, a service you can start that meets a market need or a skill that you can leverage, there are many ways. The key is to identify an area where passion and profitability can intersect. You need to take the time to consider and research this phase, as the chosen venture will require significant time and energy outside of regular employment, and because most people do not want to work 8 hours a day and after that work some more, if you are willing to put at least 1-2 hours a day towards something after work, you will be ahead of most people.

When considering ask yourself the following questions:

1) Is this something I can see myself doing over the next 5 years?
2) Is this something I am capable of learning?
3) How long will it take to grow this and see results?
4) How scalable and how far can I take this?
5) Is the overtime investment something I can sustain?

Step 3: Balancing a Job and Side Hustle (1-3 years)

Once you find a side endeavor that is worth pursuing, you need to manage your full-time work while at the same time nurturing your side hustle. This is when sacrifice will come into play; you may need to spend less time with friends, going out less, spend less time with social media, play fewer video games, cut streaming services like Netflix, etc. Remember the following: *"If we don't sacrifice for our goals, our goals become the sacrifice."* You need to enter into a stable routine that allows for growth in the side hustle using the stability provided by the full-time job. You will be in this situation for a few years until you start seeing the fruits of your labor pay out the way you want it. You need to be on the path of progress and gradually scale you venture overtime. You are going to need patience, consistent effort, adaptability, and a willingness to learn from both successes and setbacks to make sure you are getting somewhere.

Step 4: Proper Financial Management

Efficiently managing your finances becomes increasingly important when juggling a job and a side hustle. You need to allocate funds wisely between personal needs and the growth of the side project. Do not worry about profiting right away, at the beginning the side hustle will require more investment than anything. You need to grow it and get it to a point where profit is happening which will take some time. The money that comes in, at first, you will reinvest back into the business to fuel its growth. (And typically you cannot do this without a job)

Step 5: Transitioning to Full-Time on Your Venture: (After 2-3 years in)

Once you have been working on your side hustle for a few years, if you get to the point where you are starting to make some consistent money month after month and it is profitable you can start thinking about transitioning to go full-time on it. The transition should be based on both financial stability and the readiness of the business or whatever career you choose.

Some indicators of the right time to transition are the following:

- Your side hustle is not only making about the same amount of money as your current job but also provides a consistent and reliable income stream. Consistency in earnings is key, as it demonstrates the viability and stability of your business.

- Your business's profit margin should be enough to cover your basic living expenses. (Rent, Food, Transportation). Remember you are leaving your day job, so the other income will be gone. So it goes beyond just matching your current salary; it means your business income should be able to sustain your lifestyle without financial strain. (The lower your expenses are, the faster you can do this).

If it is a business that you are growing a solid customer base is a clear sign that there's a demand for your product or service. But more than just having a number of customers, you should look for growth and engagement. Are you acquiring new customers regularly? Are your existing customers returning and possibly referring others? A growing customer base indicates market acceptance and the potential for continued expansion.

- Robust Business Plan for Future Growth: You need to have a plan for what the next steps are. This plan should outline clear strategies for expanding your customer base, increasing revenue, managing costs, and dealing with potential challenges. It should also include goals and milestones to help track your progress and make informed decisions.

- You must be mentally prepared to transition from full-time time at your time to full-time entrepreneurship. It is a totally different world. Are you prepared for the uncertainties and challenges of running a full-time business? It's important to assess your emotional readiness and ensure you're equipped to handle the stress and demands of entrepreneurship.

Here's a simplified summary of the five steps to achieving financial independence:

- ***Secure Stable Income with a Job:*** This is to ensure a reliable flow of income to cover basic living expenses and provide financial security.

- ***Choose a Side Venture:*** Once you are somehow stable. Identify and begin a side project or hustle that aligns with your interests or skills. Something that can eventually supplement your primary income.

- ***Balance Job and Side Hustle:*** Manage your time and resources to maintain both your full-time job and your side venture without compromising either. Gradually build and grow your side venture through strategic planning, market research, and reinvestment of profits, especially at the beginning.

- ***Manage Dual Income Streams:*** Handle your finances wisely by budgeting your earnings from both your job and side hustle, reinvesting in your venture, and saving for the future.

- ***Transition to Full-Time Venture:*** When your side project becomes sustainable and generates consistent income, consider shifting your focus to make it your full-time endeavor.

And after this, enjoy your financial independence when your life is on your own terms. ***This can take on average 3-5 years***, depending on what you choose, your persistence, and your intelligence.

Understanding Wealth Positioning

To be able to generate wealth you need to find where to be, in other words where to "position" yourself.

Positioning refers to the strategic placement of oneself, a business, or an investment within a particular market or location where there is a substantial flow of money. It's about identifying and situating yourself in an area of the economy that is experiencing growth, demand, or increased investment.

Basically being in a place where money is circulating, so it can circulate thru you.

It is not just about physical location; it encompasses being in an industry/ sector, where money flows within and there is an influx of capital. If you are where the money is, you're strategically placed to capture and grow wealth.

Now you may be saying. *"this sounds great and all but how do I do this?"* Well is a process that involves

- Research (Understanding where money is flowing)
- Knowledge acquisition (Having the right skills, knowledge, and mindset to capitalize on the opportunities)
- Action: (Based on your research and skills)
- Adaptability (Every market is in constant change)

To give you options of the many things you can do. I have another book, it is called: **"ChatGPT is a Money-Making Machine".** In that book I lay out a lot of different opportunities where money does flow and there is capacity for growth and I teach how you can use AI (ChatGPT) to scale faster.

If you are interested in checking it out, visit my author profile on Amazon and you can find it there. What I do in that book is I break down many different businesses and opportunities that are going to still be relevant in 2030 and beyond, I explain these business in simple terms that you can understand and I provide you the many different ways to use the ChatGPT software to scale this business a lot faster and grow it to good numbers.

For those who don't know, ChatGPT is an artificial intelligence program developed by OpenAI that's capable of understanding and generating human-like text based on the input it receives. It can engage in discussions on a wide range of topics, provide information, answer questions and write anything you would like it to write. Feel free to check it out I am sure you will find it valuable.

Here is a picture of the cover for you to recognize it:

I wrote this book with the average person in mind who wants to start and online business and can use AI to scale a lot quicker. Those who are aware of the potential of AI and ChatGPT and they want to learn how to make an income, but they don't know where to start.

I am going to provide you a few bullet points that it covers so you are aware of the many different businesses are listed there:

- Various Plugins and Extensions: Discover the utility of various tools to enhance your use of ChatGPT.

- Unique Business Examples: Real-life examples of successful online businesses that can leverage AI to scale quickly
- Personalized Business Search: Learn techniques to identify and evaluate online business opportunities tailored to your skills, interests, and market trends.
- 7 Life-Altering Hacks: The hacks are specific ways and tools to enhance your productivity, transform your life and improve your lifestyle. They have the power to revolutionize your life.
- Extensive Prompt Examples: We provide a diverse collection of prompt examples meticulously curated for various aspects of progress.
- Master Prompt Creation: on top of the examples, you get a practical guide for creating effective prompts, including handling lengthy and complicated ones for different aspects of life and business.
- Grasp AI's Impact on Our World: Gain a deep understanding of the transformative role of AI in our lives
- Adapt AI to Life's Many Facets: Discover comprehensive strategies to integrate ChatGPT and AI into different aspects of life (Business, learning productivity, and creativity)

Learning an online business and using and taking advantage of AI to scale if will be one of your fastest options to build something for yourself. Many of the online business you probably heard of will be covered in this book. A lot of online business where typically you have to put a lot of work you can actually simplify a lot of the proces, and you know what? You are still early because most people are not using and that is still new, came out barely in November of 2022.

Smart Move: How Living Abroad Can Boost Your Business Journey

If you find yourself in a situation where:

- You are single
- You work from home
- You can easily move around
- You are growing an online business
- You have some money saved up
- You have a job, you work from home and you believe you can take it abroad

Relocating to a country with a lower cost of living at least for a little while can be an effective strategy for easing the transition from a side hustle to full-time entrepreneurship a lot faster.

Countries with a lower cost of living allows you to get more bang for your buck, and reduce your monthly expenses. This can be particularly beneficial if your business income is not yet stable or high enough to cover expenses in higher-cost countries like the U.S., Canada, or the UK. Expenses like housing, food, and healthcare can be significantly lower in countries like Mexico or Argentina for example.

Let's Illustrate:

Let's say you're single and you are an aspiring entrepreneur trying to grow an online side business. It's showing promise, you are making some money but hasn't yet reached its full profitability. You've been diligent with your finances and have managed to save some money, let's say you saved $2,500 USD and your expenses are not that high. This situation presents a unique opportunity, especially considering the high cost of living and financial pressures in your current location.

Let's say that you live in an average US city. Where your cost of living is around $2500 per month. What if you decide to relocate to a more affordable city in Mexico for a few months, where living costs are significantly lower than in many parts of the United States and you can live a lot cheaper. In Mexico, it's possible to find comfortable and safe apartments in the range of $300-500 USD per month. By paying several months of rent upfront, you not only secure your living situation but also free yourself from the monthly pressure of rent expenses. This move drastically reduces your living costs, allowing you to stretch your savings further and focus more financial resources and time on growing your business.

With the reduced cost of living, your $2,500 can cover much more than just housing. It can sustain your day-to-day expenses, like groceries, utilities, and internet, which are also generally cheaper in Mexico compared to the U.S. Let's say that you consider this for 3-6 months. This financial buffer provides peace of mind, allowing you to concentrate fully on your business without the immediate stress of generating a high income to cover living expenses. There is a lot you can do in a few months of full-time focus on something. More than just the financial benefits, living in a new country can be a rich cultural experience, offering fresh perspectives and possibly even new business ideas or insights. You can also meet new people, and make valuable connections adding to your social capital which we will get to in later in the book. This change in environment will also spark your creativity and help you see the world from a broader perspective, which is a valuable asset in entrepreneurship.

With the rise of digital entrepreneurship and remote work, it's now more feasible than ever to run a business from anywhere in the world. This flexibility allows entrepreneurs to choose their location based on cost of living and lifestyle preferences, rather than being tied to a specific geographic location for employment.

The US-Mexico was just an example. Depending on where you live you may want to consider different options. Colombia, Argentina. There are so many different options and countries with a low cost of living. With this strategy, the journey to financial independence can be shorter because your operational costs are lower and this allows for greater risks and investments in your entrepreneurial endeavors.

In most countries in South America, you can easily live with $1000 a month including, rent bills, transportation, and entertainment. So if you see that you are in a position where you can move out and experience being a few months in a different country it can be a very rewarding experience while at the same time, you can save money on living expenses and dedicate full-time to your side hustle if it is online. If you can move a remote job from the US to these countries, even better.

Skills, Contribution, Impact and Compensation

What I want to cover in this section is the concept of "value exchange" and how you as a whole (Who you are as a person) and your contribution to the world is typically tied to financial compensation. The more valuable a skill or service is perceived to be – in terms of rarity, demand, and impact – the higher the financial reward it garners. This relationship between skill and compensation is evident across various sectors, from technology and healthcare to arts and education. This is also very true when it comes to the workforce and the professional world. The compensation one receives is often directly proportional to the perceived value of their contribution to a business, client, or community.

Whether we realize it or not, we are constantly engaged in transactions with the world, especially in the context of our professional lives. When working in a job, the transaction is quite straightforward: we exchange our skills, time, and effort for financial compensation. This is a transaction you are making. This exchange is based on the value that our skills and contributions bring to an employer or client.

To increase our income or make more money, the focus then shifts to enhancing the value of our transactions with the world. And you do that by elevating your value and increasing the impact of your contribution to your market. The greater our positive impact is, the more we will get compensated on.

And when I say impact, I refer to the extent to which your products or services positively affect your customers and the market. High-impact businesses typically solve significant problems, fulfill unmet needs, or introduce innovative solutions that change the way people live or work.

Let's take a look at the following example:

Flipping burgers at McDonald's might seem like a straightforward task with a limited impact, as it's a job many can perform, leading to relatively modest compensation. Conversely, if you're in the business of selling homes, you're directly contributing to an essential aspect of people's lives by providing them with a place to live. This is why a worker at Mcdonalds makes less money than a real estate agent. The real estate agent role carries a greater impact, it demands a more specialized skill set, including a deep understanding of the real estate market, proficient negotiation abilities, and a thorough knowledge of the legal and financial intricacies involved in property transactions.

The principle is clear:

> **"Minimal impact will result in minimal compensation; greater impact will lead to greater compensation"**

There are different ways you can do this:

- Taking on more responsibilities at your current job
- Move to a higher paying role
- Get a higher-paying job (Which implies the value provided is higher)
- Leading larger projects
- Building a Strong Professional Reputation (Social Capital)
- Solve problems for a large group of people (Starting a business)
- Acquiring In-Demand Skills

I hope by now you understand that your compensation/ how much money you make will depend largely on what you are putting out to the world. This dynamic is constantly in play, whether you're an employee, a freelancer, an entrepreneur, a business owner, etc. "You get out what you put in." (Most of the time).

But this is not the only factor that comes into play, of course, other things need to be included as well.

Consider the following:

- You don't want to get good at the wrong thing:

Your offer must align with what the market needs or values. In other words, you need to do something that is relevant. For instance, having a niche skill like fixing broken pens might be impressive, but if there's no significant demand for it. If a pen breaks, most people will just buy a new one, they are cheap and no one thinks about that. It won't translate into substantial financial compensation.

- Align with Market Needs:

To ensure your business or skill is making a substantial impact, align your business goals with what your market needs. This alignment means understanding your customers deeply, staying tuned to market trends, and being ready to adapt your products or services to meet evolving demands.

- Hard Work vs. Smart Work:

They are both important. But there's a common misconception that working harder (Hustle culture) directly correlates with higher pay. You need to work hard, especially at the beginning, but smart work always beats hard work. It's not just the quantity of work you put in, but the quality and impact of that work that will matter the most. You can put the hard work in the wrong place and it wont matter how hard you worked.

- Visibility

No matter how impactful your skills or business might be, they can't achieve their full potential without visibility. Today's marketplace is crowded and noisy, so being seen and heard is critical. Visibility ensures that your target audience is aware of what you offer, understands its value, and knows how to access it. You need to be able to communicate your value so you are ABLE to make an impact.

- Access to Opportunities through Relationships

Building up on the last point, many times *it is not what you know is who you know*. Often, opportunities come not from your skills or knowledge alone, but through the people you know. These individuals can provide referrals, recommend you for positions, or introduce you to key players in your industry. There is something called *"Social Capital"* Which you don't hear about it often enough, this refers to the benefits you gain from your relationships with others. We are going to be expanding on this later in the book.

So as you see, who you are as a whole, what you are doing and putting out into the world, every day, month to month, year after year is what determines where you are and will be in life. If you pay attention, where you are now is the result of years of decisions and things that you have done, **and did not do**.

Something important to remember is that you need to let time catch up to what you are doing, because even when we're doing all the right things, success, impact, and recognition often don't happen quickly. The rewards of your hard work might not be apparent right away. Give it time to grow and flourish. The fruits of our labor, the rewards of our skills and contributions, often require time to manifest.

Your lifestyle Must Enhance Your Progress, Not Obstruct It

When it comes to your long-term goals, you are not going to able to achieve them if your lifestyle is not contributing to it. You must prioritize having a lifestyle where it enhances your path to your ultimate goal. This is crucial to escape the situation you find yourself in. Whether we realize it or not most people are caught in a cycle where their lifestyle, dictated by consumer habits, everyday actions, and daily spending of time and money holds them back from achieving their goals. So people want to go one way, but the way they live is directing them the other way. This is unfortunate because if they would just remove the things about their lifestyle that are not contributing they would be in a much better situation that they are in.

You need to know what is going on with your life and have the self-awareness of what you ARE, and are NOT doing. Take a deeper look at your lifestyle overall, primarily on where most of your time and money are going. The way you manage these two key resources will significantly influence your path to achieving goals.

I am going to provide you with different points on how you should approach your time and your money:

Understand the Difference Between Needs and Wants:

There are things that you NEED to spend money on and things that you WANT to spend money on,

Needs are necessary for survival and basic comfort (housing, food, healthcare, clothing, etc). Wants, on the other hand, are things that can enhance our lives but are not essential, like luxury items, entertainment, dining out, etc.

I can assure you that if you take a look at your spending you are spending a lot of money on things that really do not contribute to your life. You need to recognize this difference and decrease the spending on your wants, remember what we said about sacrifice earlier. At least until you are in the position to be able to give you these treats from the fruits of your labor you need to cut out unnecessary spending. This can help you in shifting your focus whether time or monetary on the things that really matter in your life.

If You Can: Downsize the Big 3 (Rent, Food, Car):

These 3 are the biggest expenses you will have. Unfortunately, often they take of all of your income and budget. Downsizing these can significantly impact your financial health. Consider more affordable housing options, if you can, downsize to a smaller house or apartment. If you are able to, have a roommate. If your lease ends and if are paying too much in rent, do not renew it, consider moving to a cheaper/smaller place. When it comes to food expenses, eat out less, and cook more. Regarding transportation, if you have an expensive car, big mistake, try to get a cheaper vehicle. By reducing these major expenses, you can free up a lot of money to have more for other things. You need to get the mentality that if you don't make a lot of money you cannot rent expensive places, own expensive cars, clutter your home buying stuff, and eat out too often.

When it comes to your time here CTA (Call To Action)

STOP Wasting So Much Time on Social Media, Netflix And Video Games

If you track how much time you spend scrolling on Tiktok and other social media platforms, playing video games, Netflix, and other streaming services you are going to get disgusted at yourself. Time is more valuable than money, as we covered earlier, money we can get it back, but time, we cannot.

We all have a limited amount of heartbeats. You are not going to live forever. Let's say that you spend 20 hours a week with unproductive activities. Imagine if you would spend all of that time in activities that propel you towards your goals. You would be there much faster.

I am not saying you cannot ever relax and do that a little bit, the problem is when you make it your lifestyle, you need to feel like you EARNED your leisure time because you have been working on things. And you will notice that you will enjoy these things even more. Challenge yourself to reduce these nonproductive activities into the activities that enhance your path to your ultimate goal. When you play that videogame or watch that movie after a productive day, you enjoy it a lot more.

Remember what we covered earlier. We live in an every man for himself/ survival of the fittest economy. These elites do not care about you. If you haven't noticed already, your government rarely passes any type of initiative or policy that favors the people. It is up to you to get out of the system. ***We depend solely on what we can make happen for ourselves***.

The system already makes it hard enough for us to leave. Do not make it harder on yourself.

CHAPTER 2:

From Nothing to Something

Understanding The Starting Point:

So you want to leave your paycheck to paycheck situation and enter into financial stability. Well most people do. The first step is recognizing where you currently stand, not only from a financial standpoint but your overall reality:

- Your health
- Your relationships
- Your income
- Your skills
- Your goals
- Your desired lifestyle
- Your current financial situation

You **need** to get yourself into a path of progress. Take a look at your own life and analyze where you are standing and what resources, skills, and opportunities you currently have.

- What are you doing with your days?
- Are you working?
- What are you doing after work?
- Do you have a business, a career, dreams, hobbies, or goals?
- Do you have a social circle that is fulfilling?
- What type of lifestyle do you want to have 5 years from now?
- What about 10 years from now?
- Are you healthy?
- Are you in shape?
- Do you work out?
- Are you saddled with debt?
- Do you have a stable income?
- What are your monthly expenses?
- What skills do you possess that can be leveraged for financial gain?
- Do you know what you want to do with your life?
- Are you actively pursuing any long-term careers or goals?
- What is your desired lifestyle?

Earl Nightingale said, ***"Success is the progressive realization of a worthy goal or ideal"*** meaning that as long as you know where you are, you know where you are going, and you are constantly moving in that direction you can consider yourself successful. Success is progress towards your ideal.

Every bit of progress is a success in its own right. as long as we are actively working towards our aspirations, regardless of the pace or the immediate outcomes, we are succeeding

If you are reading this book you probably fall into the following category:

- You have a job that you don't like it that much
- You are probably in debt and have very little money left after paying all your bills

How do I know this, because this is the financial loop that unfortunately most people are in. You are not the only person who struggles financially. In fact you are in the majority. Realizing this can bring a sense of relief and perspective because you know that you are not alone in this struggle. Many if not most people are grappling with similar challenges.

It is simple: Your daily activities need to align with where you want to be in five or ten years from now. You don't need to have all the answers, you just need to show up and do our best, every day, That's it. That's 80 percent of what we need to do. Remember, progress is what's important, not perfection.

What You Want Out Of Life?: Envisioning Fulfillment

Do you want to be a millionaire? A billionaire? Most people will answer NO to this question and instead say that they just want to be making enough money to be comfortable in life, do what they want to do, live life on their terms and not have to worry about money, which you don't need to be a millionaire to be in that situation.

To embark on this journey of self-discovery, individuals should begin by asking themselves some profound questions:

What does a fulfilling life look like to you?: You need to visualize the type of lifestyle you want to have, because remember, money is NOT the goal, it is only a tool to achieve your desired lifestyle.

Where Do I Want to Live?: This is important. Do you see yourself living in the place you are now for the rest of your life? Is it really the type of community and environment you desire?

What Do I Want to Be Doing?: What does your ideal day look like to you? What type of profession do you want to have? Visualize the desired typical day you want in a few years.

Do I Want to Travel?: This is very important for many. A lot of people want to travel. You may want to optimize your life so you can do this more than once a year.

Do I Want Kids?: Deciding whether to have children is a major life decision that impacts nearly every aspect of life, including career choices, living arrangements, and financial planning.

After getting these answers, asked yourself the following:

What level of financial security do I need to reach these goals? Is it 5k per month, 10k per month? 1 million a month? After all, we all want the same things in life but we enjoy it differently.

Let me tell you what most people want, ***and that includes you***.

You Want To Be In Good Health: At the base of all desires is the need for good health. It is the foundation of everything, and arguably what comes first. Not only physical health free of illness but also mental well-being as well. You want emotional stability. To be able to perform well you need to feel well.

You Want Financial Stability: After being in good health you want to be able to do what you want, when you want it without constant stress or anxiety about money.

You Want A Social Circle (Your Tribe): Humans are social creatures, and having a supportive social circle is vital for our emotional and mental health. This includes family, friends, romantic relationships, and broader community connections. You want good people around you.

You Want To Enjoy What You Do: You want to enjoy and find fulfillment in what you do for a living. Life is enriched by the activities we do and the hobbies we pursue.

You Want A Sense of Purpose: Most people want to be part of something bigger than themselves and have meaning beyond their own existence.

I am not trying to get too philosophical here, I am trying to help you understand what you truly want out of your life and this will help you make better decisions. When decisions are rooted in a clear understanding of one's desires and goals, they are more likely to lead to fulfillment. You don't want to be "successful" on paper only. You want to have all the pillars of the good life **"Health, wealth, Love and Happiness"**

The Need To Stick To Something:

> **"Stick to something for one year and see what happens"**

As we mentioned before, we live in a world where social media platforms, like TikTok, Instagram, and Facebook, among others, have painted 'quick success' as something common and have fostered instant gratification-seeking behavior in people. By now you should know not to buy into the hype and that finding true financial independence and building wealth is a process that unfolds over years, if not decades for the majority of us.

> **The vast majority of people do not become millionaires in their 20s**

I am not trying to be negative here, I am trying to show you the truth so you don't believe the wrong things about the world and have unrealistic expectations for yourself. This quick buck, get rich quick mentality is causing young people to go venture after venture, in search of quick results. After not seeing what they were expecting, they keep jumping to the next venture and repeating this cycle over and over again, growing in frustration and disappointment about themselves and life. They try something for a month or two, it doesn't work, and after they jump to the next thing. Over and over again.

We need to do a better job at sticking to something. The reality is that most businesses or paths out there have the capability to work IF you put the necessary time and persistence into it. Many if not most of your favorite entrepreneurs were not overnight successes; they were the result of continuous effort, in the face of setbacks and failures. Growth is often slow, and setbacks are frequent. The journey from zero to something significant is the cumulative result of daily efforts, persistence, and commitment to a chosen path. Most achievements worth pursuing require a foundation built on consistent effort and gradual progress over time to manifest.

Most people fail to identify and know the following: ***The beginning is always the hardest at anything you do.***

The beginning of any new endeavor is the most challenging phase. It is during this time that the groundwork is laid and at the same time everything is unpredictable and uncertain. You are doing something that is not familiar to you, so it is normal to have uncertainties. In the beginning is when you put in considerable effort without immediate results so it's the period where the investment of time, effort, and resources is high, but yet the rewards and outcomes are not yet visible. This happens because you are starting something that until recently was non existent and time has to catch up to what you are doing.

Since we can only feel and perceive what we are living right now. It is easy to become frustrated or disillusioned when you're in the thick of the struggle. Not often realizing that we are just EARLY IN THE PROCESS and if we keep going through patience, persistence, and perseverance can lead to significant achievements and successes in the future. Most people are not aware of how accomplishments work, they get tired of it. And quit.

Do the opposite. If you find a career path that you think is worth pursuing and you see a future with it, detach yourself from the outcome and go into the mindset of being there for at least 1 year before moving on to something else. You are going to face challenges, obstacles, and even failures. And you know what, that is totally normal. Getting yourself into a venture without knowing if it is going to work is part of business.

Having said all of this, it is also important to recognize when a change of direction is necessary. Being able to stick to something doesnt mean to keep doing what doesn't work, it is totally normal to fail at the first few businesses, someone tries, in fact many of your favorite business people failed at their first business they tried. Many times we find out that what we have been trying to do it wasn't really for us and that's ok. Moving along into something else and finding success in your second or third business endeavor is normal. Stopping for a little while because life gets in the way, and trying again later, is also normal. What is not normal is trying 10 different things in a short period of time, moving on to the next thing over and over again, and not sticking to anything. You are not going to achieve anything like that. We need to do a better job of having patience in what we are doing, understanding better what we are getting ourselves into, and sticking to it for longer periods of time. Persistence and commitment are key, and so is the ability to adapt and reassess. You need to learn to be flexible enough to adapt to new circumstances as they emerge and understanding that an obstacle is normal and not a reason to give up.

> **"The temptation to give up is the greatest right before you are about to succeed"**

The moments of greatest difficulty and doubt frequently precede breakthroughs and success. Typically we are trying something for months or even years without seeing much results, we have been putting time, sweat, and tears into something, for a very long time, and the urge to surrender is at its peak, it might be a sign that one is closer to their goal than they realize. Just the self-awareness of knowing how this works will make a significant difference in your journey. Self-awareness helps you navigate through challenges and uncertainties with ease since you know how something works and what to expect. Sometimes, the journey is about exploration, trial, error, and self-discovery- learning what works, what doesn't, and most importantly, what aligns with your skills, passions, and life circumstances.

The Interplay of Skills and Beliefs:

Our belief system plays a significant role in how we live our lives and ultimately where we end up. Beliefs shape our perceptions, influence our decisions, and drive our actions. The relation between what we believe we are capable of and what is possible are the two main factors for determining the paths we choose in life and how far we go down those paths. Our skills and beliefs are interlinked in a dance that can propel us forward or hold us back.

Skills are the tools and abilities we acquire through experience and education, but our beliefs are the lens through which we see the world and view our potential to use these skills effectively. Our beliefs also shape our perception of what is achievable. If we believe that certain goals or dreams are out of our reach, we may never attempt to pursue them, regardless of our skill level. We may be super capable of achieving something but our beliefs will make us not attempt it. See how powerful our beliefs are?

So we know that these beliefs can be either empowering or limiting. Unfortunately for most people, their beliefs are holding them back, not helping them. These limiting beliefs typically hold you back more than your actual skills on the matter; they also can become self-fulfilling prophecies. When we believe we can't achieve something, we are less likely to put in the effort required, thus ensuring our failure or lack of progress, which in turn reinforces the original limiting belief. So, the impact of these beliefs is often more significant than the actual deficit in skills.

<u>Different limiting beliefs you may tell yourself:</u>

"I'm not smart enough"
"I can't handle this"
"I'm not cut out for this"
"I don't have enough money to do this."
"I can't succeed because of my gender/age/race."
"It is not possible"
"I can't do this"
"I'm Too Old (or Young) for this"
 "I'm Not Experienced Enough"
Etc., etc., etc...

As we discussed before, you are **NOT** going to be good at something when you first try it, because you have never done before. Think about it:

When was the last time that you did something for the first time, and you were really good at it, right from the start? Probably it doesn't happen to you often, does it? And the more difficult that is, the more you are going to suck at it.

Think about every time you did something new; likely, you weren't an expert right off the bat. We will not be good at something when we are first trying it because it is not familiar to us, but that doesn't mean we will never be. You probably have plenty of examples where you are good at something now, but when you first tried it you were terrible at it. Every new skill or venture comes with its learning curve.

Let's reframe this: Instead of saying "I can't," change it to "How can I?". Switch the negative affirmation

"I'm not smart enough," = "I can probably learn more in this area."
"I can't handle this," = "How can I handle this?"
"I'm not cut out for this" = "What do I need to learn more about this?"
"I don't have enough money to do this." = "How can I afford this?"
"I'm Not Experienced Enough" = "Every master was once a beginner"

Unfortunately, getting rid of these beliefs tends to be harder than acquiring new skills, meaning it is typically harder to change your mindset than to acquire the specific skill. In contrast, beliefs, especially limiting beliefs, are internal and often subconscious. They are formed over time through a combination of personal experiences, cultural background, societal messages, and life circumstances so getting rid of them is hard because you have to rewire your brain.

As you can learn to replace these limiting beliefs with empowering ones, you open yourself to a world of opportunities. You become more willing to embrace challenges, learn new skills, and seize opportunities, thus unlocking your true potential. This may take time but shift your mindset little by little and trust your capabilities a bit more.

The reality is the following: Skills can be acquired, the more your level of skills the more competent you will be in an area.

I am sure you have heard the saying before "Perception is reality" and that is in fact true. Who you are as a whole influences what you do and don't do every day which has a direct impact on our daily lives and makes your reality. This relationship between perception and reality is a fundamental aspect of human experience. If we perceive the world as a place of opportunity and growth, we are more likely to take actions that align with this view, on the other hand, if our perception is one of limitation and fear, we might avoid taking risks or trying new experiences, which can lead to a very different set of life outcomes.

These lenses directly influence everyday behavior and the decisions we make – from small to bigger decisions. For example, our perception of our own abilities can determine whether we apply for a certain job, embark on a new project, or pursue a personal goal. Similarly, how we perceive others can affect our relationships and interactions, shaping our social and professional lives. Our choices are heavily influenced by how we perceive the risks, benefits, and values associated with different options.

So the reason why OUR perception is OUR reality is because it actively constructs our reality. It encompasses not only what we see but also how we interpret and make sense of it.

This means that changing our perception can indeed make us do different things which will change our realityPerception can also be limiting beliefs, which are one of the biggest barriers to personal and professional growth. These beliefs are the narratives we tell ourselves about who we are, what we are capable of, and what we deserve. They often come from past experiences, societal conditioning, or negative feedback we've internalized. Common examples include thoughts like "I'm not good enough," "I can't succeed in this field,", etc.

These beliefs are most of the time wrong, because with proper training and practice you can do pretty much everything. Just because you are not good at something at the beginning doesn't mean you will never be. We cannot allow this to happen, if something is going to hold us back it cannot be us. So you have to learn to adapt to new perspectives and challenge some of the limiting beliefs you have.

> ***Competence leads to confidence which leads to accomplishments***

This means that your confidence comes in proportion to how competent you are in something. When you have the necessary skills, knowledge, and ability to do something effectively. You are competent, and that makes you confident of what you are doing. As competence grows, so does confidence. Confidence here isn't just a feeling of self-assurance; it's a byproduct of knowing that you are capable based on your skills and past experiences. Competence fosters confidence. When you're confident in your abilities, you're more likely to take on challenging projects, make bold decisions, and persist in the face of obstacles. This proactive and determined attitude paves your way towards achievements.

If we think about it we probably were not confident we could do something that we are now able to do. The problem is that a lot of people forget that it is obvious that the first time you are going to attempt to do something you are not going to be good at it and because they are not good at it they think they will never be.

Here are some examples where people make this happen in real life:

- If you believe you're not qualified for a promotion, you might not apply for it or might perform poorly in the interview due to a lack of confidence. When you're not selected, this reinforces the belief that you weren't good enough, even though it was the lack of confidence, not competence, that held you back.
- Someone who believes that they are not meant to be financially successful may not take steps to improve their financial literacy, invest wisely, or seek better job opportunities. Consequently, their financial situation may not improve, reinforcing their belief about their financial destiny.

- Health and Fitness: An individual who believes they can never lose weight or get fit might not stick to their exercise or diet plans consistently. When they don't see results, it reinforces their belief that it's impossible for them to achieve their fitness goals.

You probably realized how bad this can be for your own advancement. we've discussed extensively how the system doesn't facilitate your journey toward achieving your goals. However, it's crucial to understand that you can be your own worst enemy and the most significant obstacle in your path.

The State Of "Flow":

A state of flow is crucial to be in a path of progress. When I say "State of flow" I mean the following:

> **When you're in flow: You know where you are, you know where you are going and you are constantly moving in that direction**

So you are not in a state of "limbo" where every day passes, nothing happens and you are lost. You are actively moving towards your goals and aspirations with a clear sense of direction and purpose. Essentially is about being in a state of progress.

In contrast, not being in flow often means feeling stagnant or stuck, lacking a clear sense of direction or purpose. You don't know where you are or where you are going in life. You are just passing through time. A lot people live this way.

When you're not in a state of flow, you might feel like you're in the same endless loop, feeling stuck, not advancing towards anything and this leaves you with feelings of frustration, dissatisfaction, emptiness and even confusion about what you are doing with your life and where you're heading.

On the other hand, when you are in a state of flow, you feel a sense of momentum and accomplishment, even if progress is slow, you feel more in control of your life and confident in your ability to reach your goals. You feel like things are happening and you are heading somewhere.

I will break this down for you with examples

Not Being in Flow:

- Lack of Clarity: Uncertain about goals or what you want to achieve.
- Stagnation: Little to no progress in personal or professional development.
- Disengagement: Low interest or motivation in daily tasks or activities.
- Inflexibility: Difficulty adapting to changes or new circumstances.
- Sense of Frustration: Feelings of dissatisfaction or unfulfillment.
- Static Learning: No active pursuit of new knowledge or skills.

- Poor Time Management: Struggling to use time effectively, often feeling unproductive.
- Negative Outlook: Pessimism or lack of confidence about the future.

Being in Flow:

- Clear Direction: You have a well-defined goal or set of goals.
- You're progressing: Regardless of pace, you are consistently taking steps towards achieving these goals.
- Clear Vision: You know what to do every day.
- You don't go with the flow, you set the flow.
- Engagement and Focus: Deep involvement in tasks and activities related to goals.
- You're Adaptable: You can adjust to circumstances
- Sense of Fulfillment: You are feeling good in your everyday life.
- Continuous Learning: Seeking and embracing opportunities for growth and improvement.
- Time Management: Effectively allocating time to prioritize goal-oriented tasks.
- Positive Mindset: Maintaining optimism and a can-do attitude, even in the face of challenges.

Recognizing when you are not in a state of flow is easy and is the first step toward changing your situation. Identifying what's holding you back, and action through consistent effort is what is going to make the shift towards a state of flow.

The self-awareness and clarity that you are getting by reading this book will help you to achieve this state, keep reading and gaining more information about these things.

The Compound Effect of Consistent Action:

Compounds mean when something builds upon each other.

> **Small, consistent actions, when compounded over time, can lead to significant and often surprising outcomes. They look small at the time, but they stack to huge things in the long run.**

When you consistently work on something, each effort builds on the previous ones. That means that with each effort, you're not starting from the same place as before; you're starting from a slightly advanced position. Over time, these small advancements accumulate, and because you're building on top of what was achieved before, the overall progress can grow exponentially rather than linearly.

Everything big was once small.

This principle can apply to most things in your life. Every action, no matter how small, contributes to building something larger over time. It's the concept that our actions, when consistently applied, stack upon each other, creating a cumulative effect that can lead to significant achievements.

Continued actions create momentum, making further progress easier and faster, similar to a snowball growing as it rolls downhill.

And this can get bigger and bigger the more input you put into it. The more time and effort you dedicate to consistent actions, the larger your results become. This exponential growth is a key feature of the compound effect. As you continue to build upon your previous actions, the potential for progress and achievement doesn't just add up—it multiplies. I am telling you this for you to take dimension of how action and achievement works so you are not disappointed when things don't happen as quickly as you would expect and for you not to fill discouraged when doing things and thinking they're nothing. Each small step you take might not seem like much on its own, but over weeks, months, and years, these steps can add up to a considerable distance. The principle works quietly and slowly; its impacts are cumulative and often only become noticeable after a considerable period.

This can take place in both directions, good and bad. When you see yourself in a bad situation, it is probably not the result of one single bad decision but a series of poor choices made consistently over time. The longer these negative habits are maintained, the more ingrained they become and the more challenging it is to reverse their effects.

So now you know how achievement and making something happen works. All of this knowledge is going to plant a seed of self-awareness in your mind and it is going to propel you to persist toward challenges instead of giving up easily when obstacles arise.

Transforming yourself takes longer than building wealth

Something important to consider when it comes to growing a business or starting a new endeavor is that it may not take as much time to grow, as the time that it will take someone to become the type of person they need (consistency, discipline, knowledge, mindset, etc) to grow that business/ endeavor in the first place.

Meaning if you have what it takes within you, you can achieve something a lot faster, but if you do not have it with you, acquiring it, typically takes more time than finding success.

For example, let's say you want to grow a Social Media Marketing business. If you have the right mindset, skills, and knowledge, you can grow this type of business to great numbers in just a few months through cold calling getting your first customers, outsourcing the marketing, networking, etc.

But becoming the person that you need to be to do this may take years, this is something not too many people think about.

> **You are not the person that can do that, yet.**

There is a difference between acquiring technical skills and knowledge for a business and developing the personal attributes necessary to effectively implement these skills. Following up on the example of SMMA (Social Media Marketing), you may learn quickly the mechanisms of running the business, such as mastering social media strategies, understanding client acquisition, and efficiently outsourcing marketing tasks, but transforming yourself into a person who can effectively execute these strategies is often a longer journey. You may be right into thinking that you can do something in a short period of time IF you would be exactly the type of person that needs to be to do that specific thing. But since you are not, it will take you time because you need to become.

The Dynamics of Input Equals Output

There is an impact on everything that we do and don't do. You need to be aware of the direct impact of your actions, thoughts, and habits on your life's outcomes.

Your inputs will equal your outputs

This applies to absolutely everything. For example, exercising: When we consistently input physical activity into our routine, the output is improved physical health, enhanced mood, and increased energy levels.

Similarly, when we invest time in learning and self-education, the output is expanded knowledge, skill development, and often, better career opportunities. These examples illustrate how positive inputs lead to beneficial outcomes.

The principle also works in the reverse, (Garbage in=Garbage out) Poor dietary habits serve as a clear example of this. When our input consists of unhealthy foods consumed regularly, the output is often poor health, including increased risk for chronic diseases, decreased energy levels, and a lower quality of life.

The picture above, on the left, you can see the motivated individual in a positive environment, and on the right, the contrasting scene of an individual playing video games in a less ideal setting. This visual representation emphasizes the impact of our daily actions on our overall life outcomes.

We are covering these aspects of life because while external systems play a role in shaping our existence, it is our personal actions that have a more immediate and profound influence on our lives.

Here are examples illustrating the concept of good inputs leading to good outputs, and bad inputs leading to undesirable outputs:

Good Inputs and Their Results

Input: Working on a Side Hustle

Output: Progress and Potential Financial Gain

Input: Regular Physical Exercise

Output: Improved Health and Fitness

Bad Inputs and their Results

Input: Frequent Consumption of Fast Food

Output: Poor Health and Potential Weight Gain

Input: Excessive Drinking

Output: Health Issues and Reduced Productivity

Something will come out of whatever it is that you are doing. The correlation between our actions (inputs) and the results or consequences we experience (outputs) cannot be overstated. As we discussed before, over time these actions accumulate, and their compounded effects become more evident in the form of achieved goals, realized dreams, and a well-lived life. Or, on the other hand, the opposite which is negative ramifications. The control you have over your own decisions and actions is far more direct and impactful than anything else in your life. The most significant factor in changing one's situation is the set of actions one chooses to take consistently.

Things outside of you control:

- You do not have any control over these governments or elites.
- You do not have control over whether the economy gets better or worse
- You cannot dictate global market trends or financial crises that might affect your financial stability.
- You have no say in the formulation of laws and regulations that govern individual freedoms.
- You are powerless to change the educational system's quality and accessibility that shapes future generations.

Now let's take you in the other direction, what you **DO** have control over, which impacts you even more:

- You have total control over YOUR reactions to external events and circumstances.
- You have the power to choose your attitude in any given situation.

- You are in charge of your personal goals and the steps you take to achieve them.
- You can decide how to allocate your time and energy each day.
- You have the autonomy to select the people you allow into your life and those you keep at a distance.
- You control your personal development, including learning new skills and knowledge.
- You determine your financial priorities and spending habits.
- You have the power to shape your physical health through diet, exercise, and lifestyle choices.
- You decide the values and principles by which you live your life.

Even though we exist within systems designed to favor a select few, individuals still possess the power to significantly influence their quality of life through their actions and decisions. You need to focus on what you can control (personal habits, choices, attitudes, and efforts). There is no point in dwelling on what's outside of your control. You have the power to significantly influence your life trajectory, more than anything or anyone. Be happy that the main control over your life is in your own hands. So, to improve what you are getting OUT of life, improve what you are putting IN to life. You have absolute control over your daily actions. The quality of your life is largely determined by the daily choices you make and the actions you take.

Also, keep in mind that bad things happen to everyone; the notion that wealth is a solution for all life's challenges and problems is a misconception. Problems, challenges, and adversities are an integral part of the human experience, regardless of one's financial status and income. Things such as health problems, relationship difficulties, and personal losses affect everyone. Wealth can provide comfort, security, and access to resources, but it does not exempt individuals from facing problems. In fact, with increased wealth can come a unique set of challenges and responsibilities. More money, more problems too.

Why you need Allies: The importance of Social Capital

Rarely can we get where we want on our own. In the journey of life, the more supportive a social circle you have—family, friends, colleagues, etc., often referred to as your "tribe"—the easier your life can be. This is called "Social Capital," which refers to the networks, relationships, and connections you have that can be economically valuable and contribute to your success, both professionally and personally.

Your tribe consists of the closest people around you, who genuinely care about your well-being and success and can provide support, guidance, and practical assistance one way or the other. Various types of allies play distinct and vital roles. Each brings unique benefits and perspectives that can aid in navigating life's complexities, here are a few examples:

Parents and Family Members: If you can manage to have a good relationship with your family, they often can be the primary support system.

Friends: Friends are great for emotional support, every time you get a beer with a friend or you share a BBQ with people it is a way for you to distract yourself and have a good time.

Mentors: Offer guidance, advice, and insights from their own experiences. Helpful in navigating career paths and professional development.

Business Partners: Share in the financial and operational tasks of a business, complement skills, and contribute to enterprise success.

Professional Contacts: Provide industry insights, job opportunities, and professional advice. Crucial for expanding your professional network.

Mental Health Professionals: If you have them, they provide emotional and mental health support.

Having good people around you is a form of capital because, just like financial capital, it can provide dividends in terms of information, opportunities, and support. Despite its significance, social capital is often underestimated in discussions about paths to wealth and well-being.

Social capital can be seen in everyday life examples: Every time you borrow something from someone, you get recommended for a job, someone gives you a ride, you get invited to a party, you don't have a place to stay and someone offers you one, or something happens to your benefit because of a connection you have, that is social capital in action. Often, the best opportunities are not advertised publicly. They are filled through personal networks or recommendations. Knowing the right people can open doors to job offers, business ventures, collaborations, and other opportunities that might otherwise be inaccessible. Each person in your network brings their own set of connections, potentially expanding your reach far beyond your immediate circle. This extended network can be a rich source of new opportunities and connections. Every relationship you have, whether it is with your parents, friends, or people you know, can be very valuable. Do not underestimate it or take it for granted. While your individual knowledge, skills, and experience are undoubtedly important, the value of who you know is important as well.

Progress is Not Linear:

Another important aspect of you getting what you want is understanding how progress works when it's happening. It IS NOT LINEAR, the line is much more messy.

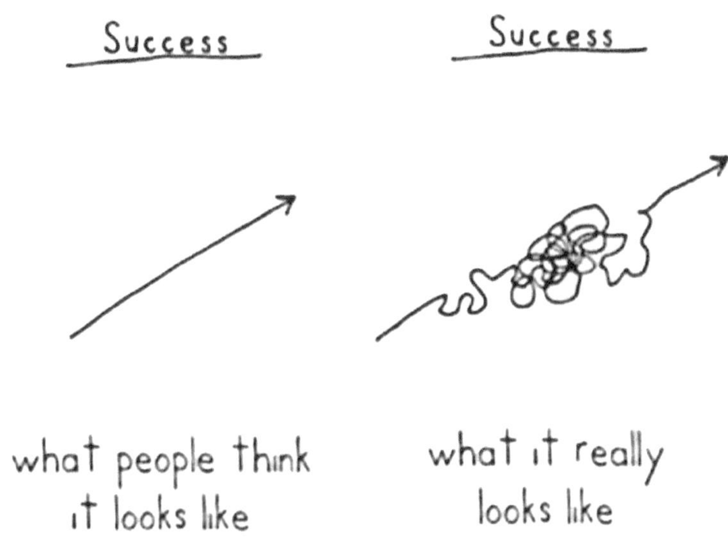

As you see the line of progress takes different twists and turns and that happens when you are dealing with obstacles, unexpected setbacks, and failures, but as long as you continue progress keeps moving forward.
So whatever you are working on you need to know that it will not be the image on the right, life will get in the way, and things will happen.

You need the following **6 components for progress to stay in place:**

- Education: To always be aware you know what you are doing and how something works
- Awareness: You need to be aware of what you are up against
- Decision: To get started with something and move along
- Action: The activities you take every day that lead to where you are going
- Consistency: You need to stay consistent in working on what you are doing to see results
- Adaptation: Life will happen, things will happen. You need to make sure you adapt to the circumstances

You need these components needed to maintain progress in motion. Each plays a distinct role in the journey towards achieving and sustaining whatever it is that you want.

Recognizing this nature of success is crucial for young adults who are too influenced by the instant gratification presented on social media. Everything that you see every day with these people living their laptop lifestyles. What many of these entrepreneurs do not show you is the years of hard work, trial, error, money lost, and all the tribulations and time it took them to be in that position. The most common scenario is for people to struggle, to take a long time to see results, to have to grind, and to have to work for months if not years to see the fruit of their labor.

So it is completely normal to encounter setbacks on your path to progress. In fact, setbacks are an integral part of the learning and growth process. Because of this reason, it is ok to shoot high and optimize for the best you can do, there is a saying that goes "Shoot for the moon. Even if you miss, you'll land among the stars." Meaning it is ok to set ambitious targets, and even if you fall short, you will still be further along than if you had aimed too low. You should optimize for the best possible outcome.

CHAPTER 3:

Financial Independence Through Multiple Avenues

What Does it mean to Financially Independent?

It is not about having a lot of money, being rich or having tons of wealth. Financial independence is basically the following:

> **"it's a state where a person has sufficient financial resources to live life on their own terms"**

That's it. It doesn't need to be more complicated than that. It's a situation where financial constraints no longer dictate your life choices and you make decisions based on preference rather than necessity. This freedom extends to all aspects of life, from daily activities to long-term plans and dreams. Financial independence also broadens choices in terms of lifestyle, such as where to live, traveling, and work that doesn't feel like work. This freedom extends to the ability to allocate time – pursuing hobbies, and spending more time on your wants without the pressure of meeting financial obligations. It doesn't mean you don't work, it means that you work on your terms.

You would be surprised that achieving this is easier than you think, This concept is often misconceived as requiring a vast accumulation of wealth, but that is not the case, it can be achievable on a much more modest scale, especially for those who embrace a simpler lifestyle. The key lies in the relationship between your income, your expenses, and your persistence in pursuing your financial goals.

For individuals who prefer a simpler lifestyle, this gets a lot easier. Since their day-to-day expenses are low, they can risk more resources on other things. With fewer financial obligations, the amount of money needed to sustain their lifestyle is less, making financial independence more achievable.

> **The simpler your lifestyle is, the easier it will be to achieve financial independence**

Let me give you an example of two people John and Jesse: John has an income of 200k per year and Jesse has an income of 50k per year, but Michael is in a lot more financial pressure than Jesse. How is this possible? Well let me explain:

John, despite his substantial $200k annual income, is under significant debt resulting from lifestyle inflation. He has multiple car payments/ insurance, an expensive mortgage, and high credit card debt from frequent purchases which have created a financial burden that his income struggles to cover, and despite making 200k per year which equals to making about 16k per month, he lives paycheck to paycheck. You would be surprised how many people are in this situation, unbelievable right?

Michael's situation illustrates an important principle: high income does not automatically equate to financial stability or wealth. Despite his earnings, Michael may find himself in a precarious financial position, with little savings or investments, and constantly under the pressure of meeting his debt obligations.

Jesse on the other hand, who earns much less, only $50k a year, which is about the average income household in the United States. He has adopted a more modest lifestyle. By choosing to live in a more affordable home, driving a less expensive car, and avoiding the trap of unnecessary spending, his expenses are significantly lower. This lifestyle choice allows him to allocate a greater portion of his income into other things. Jesse's approach demonstrates the power of living within one's means and the importance of prioritizing long-term financial health over immediate gratification. Despite earning less, Jesse is actually better off financially than John.

The conclusion of this example is that with wise choices and needing less, you can achieve a lot.

You can have a very good income but an spending problem that can leave you unstable, while on the other hand you can have less income without a spending problem and being more stable. I hope that explaining this to you opened your eyes on how realistic this can be and it is a very achievable goal to have a life of security, choice, and peace of mind.

Achieving this varies from person to person and depending of the amount of debt they have. But generally you can achieve financial independence within a few years if you do the following:

- You choose a simple lifestyle
- You work on a project and you are able to make it work
- You can move to a country where the cost of living is cheaper. (If you can do it, I understand this is not for everyone)

Traditional Employment: Use It As A Tool

In recent years, there's been a growing trend of demonizing the traditional 9-5 job, putting it as a trap or barrier to personal freedom. And of course, there is some truth about the blockage and barriers of a traditional 9-5 when it comes to financial freedom and living your desired lifestyle. But what is often left aside in this discussion is that it is necessity. You must see a traditional 9-5 job as a TOOL on your path to freedom rather than a stepping stone.

Let's bring you back to the real world, the fact is that if you were not born into a wealthy family, a job is necessary if you want to live a life of autonomy while you build something on the side for the long run. It is what it is.

You need an INCOME while you build something and you cannot build something with no money.

You need support and financial stability to allow you to take more calculated risks in other areas of life, meaning you can explore other income-generating opportunities without the immediate pressure to succeed for your livelihood. This security can foster a more creative and risk-tolerant approach to business, as the financial risk is mitigated by the stability of the regular job. We need to learn not to buy into the hype of social media pushing quick full-time entrepreneurship as something that happens quick and easy. The reality is that for most of us that will not happen and we need income and stability to be able to grow something for the long run.

I am going to touch a few points to consider..

<u>A good job/career:</u>

- **It Enables You to Grow Side Hustles:** Having a traditional job allows you to develop side hustles without the pressure of relying on them for immediate income. Since most ventures do not become profitable in the short term, a job allows you to bring income in while you grow something else. You need to feed a business or venture more at the beginning so it has the potential in the future to feed you. In the meantime, your day job sustains your daily living. Basically, it gives you stability during growth.

- **You Learn Skills and get paid for:** There are so many different things you can learn in different aspects of the economy. High-skill jobs are an opportunity to learn something new. Many of these skills are often transferable and can become assets in your future and it allow you to know deeply how a sector of the economy works from within.

- **It Provides You with Real-Life Experiences:** Summing yourself into different areas and real-life real-life scenarios can enhance your understanding of the working world. These experiences are invaluable; they provide a practical perspective on how businesses operate, how teams function, and how complex projects are managed.

- **You Have Some Benefits to Take Advantage Of:** Traditional employment often comes with a range of benefits beyond the paycheck. They may offer some good life insurance or retirement plans, or maybe they allow you to get something for free or they may offer paid vacations, etc. These benefits contribute to your current quality of life and they are worthy of being acknowledged. If you use them wisely, they can contribute greatly to personal well-being.

- **It Opens Opportunities for Meeting People and Expanding Your Influence:** A job, more than just work; can be a platform for networking and expanding your sphere of influence. Every colleague, client, and professional contact is a potential gateway to new opportunities. Let alone if you can find a group of friends there, or your significant other. It is always good to engage in the social environment of the workplace since you open doors to collaborations, insights, and ventures that might otherwise remain inaccessible.

- **High-Paying Jobs Are a Direct Path to Financial Independence:** If you are making a good income with your job, the path to financial independence can be significantly shortened. Earning let's say over $70,000 per year, gives you leverage to invest heavily in side hustles. This level of income allows for a more aggressive strategy, accelerating wealth accumulation and providing a strong financial foundation for independence. (And if you can keep a simply lifestyle with this type of income, it is a piece of cake)

- **It Helps You Build Your Credit and Get Access To The Financial System:** Establishing and building creditworthiness is a crucial element in today's financial landscape. When you have a steady income from a job demonstrates that you have a source of funds to meet your debt obligations, which is a key factor in building a strong credit profile. Having good credit is important for obvious reasons since it opens so many doors, such as better terms on loans, lower interest rates, and access to higher credit lines if you need them.

On top of this, I want to include that it can enhance your understanding of Markets. As we mentioned before, diverse employment experiences across different sectors offer a unique advantage in understanding various segments of the market and the economy. For example, let's say that you worked:

- In the car insurance industry
- In the credit card industry
- In finances
- And in retirement plans

You will probably need to use a car, a credit card, you have finances and you are going to retire one day. Do you see what I am getting at?

You have a wealth of knowledge that you can use to your benefit and take advantage of what you know when other people are more oblivious. Each role can give an understanding of how different market segments operate, and how the economy works and it may help you with your own business or ventures.

So instead of seeing a 9-5 job as an **obstacle** to meet your goals you should use it as **a tool** to meet your goals. Also, keep in mind that you can get a job that relates to your desired occupation or path. This can be an invaluable strategy for you. When your employment is in the same field as your ultimate career goals, it allows you to understand the nuances and inner workings of your desired industry firsthand. This direct exposure equips you with practical knowledge and insights that just research cannot match. You learn about the day-to-day realities, challenges, and best practices in your field of interest, which can shape your approach and vision for your future. Let along if you are also able to build a relevant professional network and connections which can serve you to advance in your industry.

Seeing employment this way is a lot more practical than seeing it as a stepping stone. Of course, we are talking about good quality jobs where you can find value for yourself aside from your paycheck. If you do not like your job and doesn't provide you with any of these things, I encourage you to get a higher quality, higher paying job so you can extract value from your employment in terms of skill acquisition, network building, financial stability, and industry insights. Anything that can significantly benefit your side projects or entrepreneurial ventures.

Instead of feeling trapped by a 9-5 job, view it as an integral part of your journey, a necessary phase for where you are right now, where you are gearing up, gathering resources, and preparing for the next big leap.

So it is a *phase of preparation*, not a *period of stagnation*.

Multiple Financial Directions

One way or another, people make choices, either actively or passively. It is challenging to quantify exactly, but it is safe to say that the majority of people live their lives in a passive way, meaning they respond to circumstances as they arise, often making decisions based on the immediate demands of the situation rather than a predetermined plan or goal. These individuals might wait for opportunities to present themselves rather than seeking them out, adapting to challenges and changes without actively influencing or anticipating them.

On the other hand, we can say that a minority of people are more proactive, meaning they are actively building their lives and taking actionable steps; they adopt a more initiative-driven and intentional approach to life. They set goals, plan their paths toward achieving these goals, and take actionable steps to make their visions a reality.

Both of these types of people make decisions, but the way they make them is different: Proactive people make decisions based on a conscious evaluation of their goals, values, and the long-term consequences of their actions. On the other hand, reactive individuals tend to make decisions in response to immediate needs or external pressures, without necessarily considering the bigger picture or long-term implications.

This world is broad and complex with a lot of different paths people can take. I am not going to break all of these down, but I will summarize them into the 3 main categories that you will likely end up pursuing in your life.

The three main roads you will likely end up:

- Higher Education and Specialized Careers
- Corporate and Industry Careers
- Entrepreneurship and Business Ownership

These are the main paths people will take in their life time. Either has its pros and cons. Let's break down each one:

<u>Higher Education and Specialized Careers:</u>

These people have a vision of their desired professional path, they have a deep interest or passion in a specific field that requires advanced knowledge and skills. The journey for this often requires higher education—be it college, university, or vocational training to achieving the career goals
 Examples of careers in this category span a wide range, including medicine, where doctors and nurses dedicate years

to study and training; law, where lawyers must thoroughly understand legal systems; academia, where researchers and professors aim to expand the frontiers of knowledge; and engineering, where professionals design and build the infrastructure of the modern world.

Typical profile:

- Personality type: Detail-oriented, appreciating the intricacies and complexities of their chosen field.
- Interests: Deeply passionate about their specific area of study or work.
- Values: Dedication to excellence and mastery in their field.
- Goals: Aspiration to reach top positions within their chosen profession.

- Examples of these careers:

    - Medical professionals (doctors, surgeons, nurses)
    - Legal professionals (lawyers, judges)
    - Academics and researchers
    - Engineers and architects
    - IT specialists and data scientists

(Likely not you reading this book)

<u>Corporate and Industry Careers:</u>

This path is where a significant portion of the workforce is. This broad category encompasses a wide range of roles across various sectors and industries, making it accessible to people with diverse educational backgrounds. The majority of them are those entering the job market simply seeking employment. This diverse sector attracts individuals from various backgrounds, many of whom may not have a specific career path in mind but are driven by the immediate need for a job or the desire for a stable income. Individuals who pursue this path often enter the job market with the aim of climbing the corporate ladder, leveraging hands-on experience, skills, and internal opportunities for advancement. The profile of these individuals is marked by adaptability, a willingness to learn, and the ability to seize opportunities as they arise.

Typical profile:

- Personality type:

    - Practical, dealing with life's challenges as they come.
    - Resilient, capable of adapting to the circumstances they find themselves in.
    - Dependable, performing their roles with consistency and reliability.

- Interests:

  - Seeking stability and a steady income through their job.
  - Interested in roles that allow for a balanced life outside of work.
  - Open to learning and taking on tasks that can enhance job security.

- Values:

  - Valuing job security and the benefits that come with steady employment.
  - Prioritizing family and personal life over career ambition.
  - Appreciating simplicity and finding satisfaction in fulfilling their job's requirements.

- Goals:

  - To maintain employment that provides for their needs and possibly those of their family.
  - To find contentment and balance between work and personal life.
  - To achieve a level of competence and security in their role, even if not seeking higher advancement.

(You are most likely in this category)

Entrepreneurship and Business Ownership:

These individuals are driven by the vision of creating and leading their lives their way. They are not not content with the status quo; they are always on the lookout for new opportunities and are willing to take significant risks to bring their innovative ideas to life. This path appeals to those who possess a strong sense of autonomy and a desire to control their destiny. They have all kinds of traits and motivations. they may have a job already but they are always exploring side projects, start-ups, or other business endeavors alongside their primary employment. They are naturally curious, always on the lookout for new trends, markets, and opportunities that could translate into successful business ideas.

- **Personality Type:**
  - Innovative and creative, constantly thinking outside the box.
  - Highly motivated and self-driven, with an inherent need to achieve and excel.
  - Risk-tolerant, willing to embrace uncertainty for the sake of potential rewards.
  - Excellent multitaskers, capable of managing various projects and commitments efficiently.

- **Interests:**
  - Deeply interested in market trends, new business ideas, and opportunities for innovation.

- Keen on personal and professional development, always looking to acquire new skills and knowledge.
- Fascinated by the challenge of creating something valuable and impactful from scratch.

- **Values:**
- Independence and autonomy in their professional life.
- Achievement and success, not just in financial terms but also in terms of impact and legacy.
- Resilience and perseverance, valuing the lessons learned from setbacks and failures.

- **Goals:**
- To build and grow successful businesses that not only generate significant income but also have a lasting impact.
- To achieve financial freedom and security, enabling a lifestyle that aligns with their aspirations.
- To diversify their professional activities, ensuring multiple streams of income and reducing dependency on a single source.

You are most likely in the following situation:

> *You have a job that they probably don't like that much, income is not as high as you would like it and you want to get ahead and do something else to make more money.*

That is most people out there. We all want better things for ourselves.

The good thing is that you have options, there are a lot of things you can do to get ahead in life, to have an overview of the options that you have I will encourage you to read the free gift that came with this book, over there you will find multiple options of career paths and things you can do inside and outside of college.

The most important thing to remember during this time is that it's okay to take your time. Rushing into decisions without proper thought and exploration can lead to choices that don't align with your true interests or goals. Take this opportunity to deeply explore what you're passionate about, what sparks your curiosity, and what you value most in life. These introspections are crucial as they can guide you towards a path that is more fulfilling and suited to your individual aspirations.

Here is the code again just in case you want to scan it and get it:

From where you are right now to where you want to be, this is generally the path you want to take:

1) Get a job to support yourself, the more money you can make the better—

While you are there..

2) Research different paths that you believe will align with your goals and skills: Do not be afraid if this takes you months:

From your research ….

3) Gather a few different options, and evaluate them in terms of the time and financial investment required for each to become successful

After this..

4) Get ready and get started. Keep your job and give your side venture 5-10 hours per week.

Turn your research and planning into tangible steps towards your new path.

The Digital Economy (Making Money Online)

Unless you live under a rock, you must know that there are a lot of online businesses out there where you can make a living. It is easier than ever to grow a side online business, especially since AI came into play. I am sure you have seen a ton of ads from entrepreneurs offering the world and the "Laptop Lifestyle" that a lot of people want to have. I am going to give you good news: This is indeed possible, you CAN make money online and you can do it relatively quickly if you know what you are doing, you take the time and you are persistent.

- Businesses do not fail, people do:

When it comes to the online business world and making money here is the reality, pretty much almost everything could work, most of them can make you very good money if you do them right. Many of them do not require a lot of capital to start, definitely less than the average price of college tuition. And in 2-3 years you could be making substantial amounts of money as long as you keep progressing. All from your computer. Yes it is possible. But just because it is possible doesn't mean it is easy. Some business will take more work than others and some will match your personality and skills more than others.

If you have individual excellence and the capacity to navigate or adapt to external conditions, you can make almost any online business work. Of course some are better than others, but maybe better isn't the right word, "different" may be a better word.

You need to take the time to reaserch different life avenues, this may take a little while but a period of reaserch is necessary if you don't know what you want to do.

Entrepreneurship Isn't for Everyone, and That's Perfectly Fine:

> *Everyone has the potential to become an entrepreneur, though not all will choose or wish to pursue it*

In today's digital age, there is a pervasive cultural and online narrative that portrays entrepreneurship as the ultimate/only path to success. You see this all over the internet across all platforms (Instagram, TikTok, Facebook, YouTube, etc).

Entrepreneurship is great, and it can be very fulfilling, and you can do great things with it. But there is something that we need to acknowledge:

It is NOT for everyone.

The internet is packed with stories of individuals achieving "Fast" success and wealth through starting their own businesses. Don't get me wrong, it does happen, and these stories can be very inspiring, but they paint an overly simplistic and many times, misleading picture of what being an entrepreneur/ owning and living off your own business really entails.

The problem is that the appeal of being one's own boss, the freedom to pursue one's passions, and the potential for substantial financial gain are highlighted, while at the same time the challenges, risks, and most importantly the time that it takes to get there are often downplayed or ignored. We hear a lot about the rewards, but not enough about the sacrifices and journey involved in getting there. This portrayal is misleading because it fails to acknowledge the hard work, the uncertainty that you face, and the potential for failure that comes with most entrepreneurial ventures. There is also a psychological component of entrepreneurship that often doesn't receive enough attention. It is just not a good fit for everyone, and not because they can't do it, it is because entrepreneurship requires a certain mindset and psychological resilience that not everyone possesses either because they just don't have it in them, or they don't want to.

Many people just don't aspire or are willing to be their own boss, and that's fine.

Keep the following in mind:

- Everyone Has Different Risk Tolerance: Entrepreneurship involves risk, whether it is financial, personal, or professional. Not everyone is comfortable with this level of uncertainty.

- The Drive And Motivation Is Not There: The drive to start and run a business often stems from a deep-seated passion or ambition. Not everyone feels this pull strongly enough to venture into entrepreneurship. For some, the motivation might lie in more stable and predictable career paths.

- Personality Traits: Certain personality traits, such as being a self-starter, adaptable, resilient, and confident, are often attributed to successful entrepreneurs. However, these traits are not universal, and not possessing them doesn't mean a lack of capability or success in other fields.

- Working a job and then some more? For many, this means working evenings, weekends, and even holidays, especially in the early stages of establishing the business. Not everyone is willing to do that.

The goal is NOT to be an entrepreneur, the goal is to achieve financial independence and you can achieve that without having to be one.

So if the idea of building your own business doesn't resonate with you, that is totally fine. There are ways to improve your life and attain financial independence without having to be a business owner. Which is great news for you.

The options you have if you do not want to be an entrepreneur but achieve financial independence is the following:

- You Need a High-Paying Job/Career:

If you don't want to build a business, fine, you still to earn an income. And for that, you need to secure a high-paying job or career.

> ***Your income is your primary wealth-building tool.***

The more you earn, the better lifestyle you can build for yourself and also the more you can allocate towards other things like investments, or paying off debt.

To maximize your earning potential, You may have to invest in learning a skill. Such as obtaining an advanced degree or professional certifications, that open doors to higher-paying positions. And remember it is not about just how much money you make, it is also about how you manage what you earn. So if you are able to secure a high income while avoiding lifestyle inflation, it can help you save and invest more of your income.

2) You Need to Make Investments on the Side:

To build wealth or achieve financial independence, you need to build something on the side. True financial independence often requires building wealth through additional channels, there is no other way. You have to do something besides your job, and investing as a viable alternative. This could involve investing in real state, putting money into retirement accounts like 401(k)s or IRAs, which offer tax advantages and compound interest over time, or other investment venues, such as stock market, mutual funds, bonds, Options, Crypto, Etc.

Remember, each of these options comes with a risk, unfortunately, to build wealth you are not going to be able to escape a side hustle of some sort and take any type of risks.

You may argue that pursuing investment or engaging in real estate can be a form of entrepreneurship in and of itself, and you would be right because it is. Doing these things require a similar mindset and initiative to start and grow them. You will need to have a high income of over 100k or more depending on where you live to achieve their long-term financial goals. The reality is that if you want it to come sooner, your income is not that high or you have too many expenses:

> **You have to do something outside of your job. If not you will stay in the system, and if you bought this book is because you want out.**

So you have to look at your capabilities, aspirations, and life circumstances. Success and financial independence can be achieved through various means, not limited to the entrepreneurial route because ultimately, the goal is not to become an entrepreneur but to achieve financial independence. How you get there. It is up to you.

Living Below Your Means: Embracing Minimalism for Financial Freedom.

> **"The less you spend on your personal life, the more you can bet into something else"**

We touched a bit into this a little bit earlier in the book, we are going to expand more in here. You have the choice to live your life however you want, but if you don't have a lot of money, you should not be spending a lot of money and living a lifestyle that is above what you can afford.

When it comes to struggling financially, living beyond one's means often the most common cause of financial trouble. For example, renting a luxurious house or driving an expensive car that significantly eats into the monthly budget are classic cases of living beyond means. These choices are very stupid because they only offer short-term gratification and often result in heavy financial burdens in the form of high monthly payments and interest accruals. This lifestyle of spending and "keeping up with the Jones" restricts your ability to invest your resources in more important aspects of life, such as creating your future. As I mentioned before your income is your most important wealth-building tool. You need to learn to minimize personal expenses to maximize other investments. Reducing your unnecessary expenses and not having too many bills to pay will free up more of your income to invest in wealth-building activities.

YOU NEED TO BE CALLED OUT:

If you make less than $45,000 per year.

You Should NOT Rent Expensive Apartments or Houses: If you don't make that much, why would you rent an expensive place?. It doesn't make sense to spend a lot of money on rent when you don't make that much money, Make sure the expenses for your rent does not exceed 30% of your income.

You Should NOT Be Driving an Expensive Car: Cars are the No. 1 wealth killer. They are typically your second biggest monthly expenses after rent. Do not buy into the hype of seeing your car as a status symbol. I understand you need to drive a car to get around. But if you are not in a position to have an expensive car, don't have one. Drive something more affordable and something that goes with your income. Because remember it is not only your car payment and insurance. Your car is a depreciating asset, that at the same time, you have to pay to maintain, (Maintenance and fuel).

You Should NOT Be Spending a Lot on Eating Out: Once in a while, not a big deal, treat yourself. But regular dining at restaurants or ordering takeout can quickly add up. Cook at home more.

You Should NOT Be Buying Expensive Household Items: If you find yourself constantly buying stuff you don't need, it is a habit that you may consider changing. Clutting your home with stuff not only will not make you happy, but it will drain your pockets and take more of your time.

Some people need to hear that. Please live and spend accordingly. You need to realize the impact of your spending habits.

There are just so many people making stupid financial decisions, As we covered in chapter one, the system doesn't make it easy for you to be financially independent, so you don't need to make it even harder on yourself. If you are broke why would you spend $1000 USD on a TV, or why are you renting a $3500 apartment, why are you driving a $50.000 car? You need to understand that this is not smart it is incredibly reckless, unsustainable, and irresponsible.

I am not saying you should not have a TV, and I am not saying you should not have a car, I am not saying you should not enjoy life. What I am saying is that you should be making choices that align with your financial situation, and make the path to wealth easier on yourself. There is nothing wrong with living within your means, it is actually very smart and a key principle for achieving financial independence. Think about it, how are you going to get ahead if you keep buying all this stuff? The idea here isn't to deprive yourself of enjoyment or the things you need. It's about making smart decisions that align with your financial reality. Your spending should align with your income.

If you're earning a modest income, you have to be mindful of where your money is going. Every dollar you save on rent, transportation, and daily expenses can be redirected toward building your future. Your financial health is more important than yout immediate gratification. For example, choosing a reliable, affordable car over a luxury model not only saves you on the initial purchase price but also reduces ongoing costs like insurance, maintenance, and fuel.

> **"We buy things we don't need with money we don't have to impress people we don't care.".**
> **Please don't be this person.**

Your focus should be on building a solid foundation for your financial future and knowing that you will need to sacrifice a bit of your lifestyle today for a better future. Do not fall into the trap of consumerism, stop buying things for the sake of status, and looking good for other people. There is really no benefit for you to try to keep up with the social expectations. What do you prefer?

    A) You being in control over your financial choices
    B) Your financial choices being in control of you

The answer is A. That's where you want to be.

What if I told you that enjoyment does not equate to spending on high-end items? Experiences with your loved ones and making life richer in memories and connections will. That is what is more strongly linked to happiness. Sooner or later, you will realize this.

What is Minimalism?:

Minimalism is a lifestyle choice that is fighting back against the consumerism prevalent in today's society. It has a focus on simplicity and the essentials in life. It recognizes the unnecessary things that clutter our lives and prevent us from focusing on what matters in life, which guess what, is not material goods.

<u>*What really matters in your life is the following:*</u>

- *Your mental and physical health,*
- *Your relationships*
- *Your life experiences*
- *Your personal and financial growth.*
- *The path of achieving your ultimate goal (Purpose)*

This lifestyle doesn't necessarily mean living with the bare minimum or being extremely frugal with everything. It means focusing on the things that add value to your life and avoiding the unnecessary clutter that fills your house, your mind, and empties your pockets. This helps you simplify your life, gives you more clarity about the world, provides more personal freedom, and makes your pursuit of happiness much easier.

Adopting minimalism into your life will improve not only your financial stability but also your mental well-being, (Less spending, more leftover for what matters).

The multiple benefits of adopting this lifestyle:

- **Reduction in spending**: One of the most obvious benefits. Less unnecessary spending means more savings, more money leftover and less debt, leading to greater financial security and freedom.

- **Reduced stress and increased contentment**: By making life simpler, minimalism significantly lowers stress levels and increases feelings of contentment.
- **Creating a sense of calm and order**: When you have fewer things to worry about and you eliminate excess, you will have more organized spaces and a more peaceful environment. This contributes to a serene and calm mindset.

- **Clearer focus on personal goals, interests, and relationships**: The less energy, time and money you spend on other things, the more of these things you will have for others. You have more mental, emotional, and financial space for what truly matters (Mental and physical health, relationships, life experiences, personal and financial growth, and your overall purpose).

- **Reduces clutter**: By reducing physical clutter in your living spaces, you will be more comfortable and it makes it easier to focus on tasks, goals, and personal values.

- **Promotes sustainability**: Minimalism often leads to consuming less, which can reduce one's carbon footprint and promote a more sustainable lifestyle.

- **Facilitates mobility and flexibility**: Having fewer possessions makes it easier to move, travel, or adapt to life changes, providing a sense of freedom and flexibility in your life. You feel so free.

- **Encourages intentional living**: When you switch your focus, you find more meaning in your life, you have a sense of purpose.

- **Boosts creativity**: A minimalist environment can stimulate creativity by limiting distractions and encouraging innovative ways to solve problems.

- **Strengthens relationships**: Believe it or not, adopting a minimalist lifestyle improves your relationships because you invest more time and energy into building meaningful relationships and experiences.

- **Enhances appreciation for what you have**: You have more of a glass-half-full mindset. You are more grateful for what you have than dwelling on what you don't have.

To end this section, You don't have to become a minimalist if that is not your thing, we all enjoy the fruits of our labor in different ways. But I want you to become aware of the trap of the consumer-driven society. The fewer resources you have the more you should adopt it and the more you have, the more you can ease up on it and enjoy the things you like because we all have our toys we like to play.

Consider adopting this lifestyle into your life, it will lead to an easier time achieving your goals and a more fulfilling life.

It's Okay Not to Have It The Answers:

We typically have more questions than answers, that's life. Especially when it comes to financial planning and life decisions, it is entirely normal not to have all the answers.

Uncertainty is a natural and unavoidable part of the human experience.
You are living day by day, and when it comes to financial paths, they are unpredictable and rarely straightforward . What if I tell you that:

Getting into a business or career path and not knowing if it's going to work, is part of the game

Not having all the answers does not equate to failure or a lack of direction. You have to embrace the uncertainty and know that obstacles and challenges will come, you just need to have the mindset of "When they do come, I'll deal with them"

The idea that successful people always have all the answers is a myth that needs debunking. The reality is that many successful individuals have navigated through significant uncertainties to reach where they are. It may seem that their journeys are marked by a seamless progression of well-laid plans, but the reality is that they got where they are by adaptability and resilience. Trust me, they had to learn from successes and failures.

You are choosing to read and educate yourself, which tells me that you are probably going to be alright. You are taking a proactive approach to learning and seeking knowledge, which is crucial for getting ahead. Education, whether formal or through self-directed learning like reading this book, equips individuals with the tools and perspectives needed to navigate through unclear waters.

CHAPTER 4:

The Education System: How You Should Approach it

What Is The Situation With The College System

It's no secret that our education system is flawed, especially when it comes to higher education (College). We are going to have a serious talk about this.

Historically speaking, education has long been a privilege of the elite. For centuries, it served as a gatekeeper of social status, with access to learning mainly restricted to the upper class, or just those who can afford it. For most of history, the notion of widespread education was virtually nonexistent; not everyone had access to it. Literacy and learning were tools that only the elites had and they used them for power and control.

But we are now in the 21st century, where education has become more widespread. At the moment, we have an education system where most people attend public schools in their early years. These systems decide your curriculum, what you are going to learn, and the timeframe of these careers. There are aspects that can be improved in our early education system, but we are going to focus here on our higher education system, which is where most of the problems start.

Whether or not you decide to go to college, you should read this section because it is going to give you a better perspective on the concept of education. I want to be clear about something. I am NOT going to tell you not to go to college; there are situations where you should probably go, and that depends on who you are as an individual, your interests, and your life circumstances. However, I want you to be aware that there are situations where college is definitely not the best option for you and could be the last place you want to go. The college system is flawed, and it is causing a many problems not just for individuals who choose to go to it but also for the economy overall.

So I have seen 6 **major problems** with the education system:

1. <u>The Cost of Education is Out of Control</u>: College education has become increasingly expensive, with tuition fees rising at a rate that outpaces inflation. This escalation in cost puts significant financial strain on students and their families, making higher education less accessible to many.

2. <u>It Neglects Entrepreneurial Education:</u> Traditional college education often focuses on preparing students for employment rather than entrepreneurship or living lives on their own terms. This neglects the teaching of crucial entrepreneurial skills like innovation, risk-taking, and business management, which are essential in today's dynamic economic landscape. And focus on just always working for someone else, which is unfulfilling for many.

3. <u>Lack of Innovation:</u> Colleges are very slow to adapt to changes in technology and the job market. They are behind decades in their teaching styles and what works in today's world. This lack of innovation is leaving students with outdated knowledge and skills.

4. <u>The Huge Disconnect Between Education and Employment:</u> College curriculums are not adequately preparing students for the practical realities of the workforce. When getting into the marketplace after long years in college, they often find a mismatch between what students learn in college and what is needed in the job market. This disconnect is leading to difficulties in finding employment related to one's field of study and contributes to underemployment, and that gets me into the following problem.

5. <u>Expensive Degrees Leading to Low-Paying Jobs:</u> Many students invest in degrees that do not lead to high-paying careers. There is a huge imbalance

between the cost of education and the potential earnings in certain fields and it is leading to financial difficulties for graduates where they have huge amounts of debt they cannot pay off. Getting to my next point

6. <u>The College Debt Crisis:</u> The high cost of college education and the problem in the above section have led to a massive accumulation of student debt, (1.7 Trillion as of 2023) which puts a huge strain not only on individuals but also the whole economy as well. This debt burden is bad for everyone.

As you have seen all of these issues affect you greatly, unfortunately, the ripple effect of the current state of higher education has broader societal implications. As individuals grapple with mounting debt and uncertain job prospects, the economy at large feels the strain.

This situation calls for a fundamental reevaluation of the role and value of higher education in our society. We need to question the long-held belief that a college degree is the only path to success.

When You Should And Should Not Go To College:

Keeping that into consideration, I am going to provide you with a few points on where you should and should not go to college, this will give you an idea if it is or isn't for you

You **SHOULD** go to college if you meet the following criteria:

- You are SURE of what you want to do because you are passionate about it and it REQUIRES a college degree to exercise the career (Doctor, Engineer Lawyer, Teacher, etc)
- The ratio of what the career will make you vs the debt you will incur MAKES SENSE. Meaning the debt will be manageable.

You **SHOULD NOT** go to college if you meet the following criteria:

- You are UNSURE what to do in life
- You are NOT passionate about a specific career or working in a specific sector
- You have a mindset where you just want to make more money and live comfortably.
- You are money or lifestyle motivated

This is a very personal decision and you should approach it with a clear understanding of what it is that you want out of life, and circumstances.

On one hand, college can be ideal if you have a definitive career path in mind and require specific academic qualifications and a degree. Fields such as science, technology, engineering, and medicine. If you want to follow any of these careers, you have to go to college, there is no other choice, and at the same time, you can take advantage of networking and the connections you can make with other professionals.

However, college is not the best route for everyone. If you find yourself uncertain about your career path or lacking a specific passion that requires a college degree, you want to explore other options. Like I mentioned before if you are motivated by financial gain or a particular lifestyle, rather than a commitment to a specific field, **DO NOT GO TO COLLEGE.**

This is not the 1950s anymore, in today's job market, and the world we currently live in, many industries, including information technology and digital marketing, place a higher value on skills and practical experience over formal academic credentials.There are a lot of high paying jobs that do not require a college degree. There are a lot of different ways to make a living online and also offline without the need for a degree. You need to understand that college is just ONE of the many different ways to make a living.
If you are a person who excels in self-directed learning, meaning you are good at learning things on your own, the structured environment of a college may not be necessary or optimal for you. The ability to self-learn has become increasingly valuable and feasible with the abundance of online resources and courses available. If you follow this route you may find that your learning experience is more flexible, and it is more practical and, and also much cheaper than going to college.

"If you have a viable business idea and the resources to execute it, diving directly into it could offer a more direct and fulfilling path to professional success than going to college"

The current system has diverged from the ideal concept of education. In the contemporary landscape, education has increasingly been treated as a commodity. Receiving a college degree is the primary focus of schooling rather than receiving a true "education.". Since the education system is flawed from the top, it creates problems everywhere else, mid to bottom.

Let's be honest: The flaws in the education system are by design, there is a corruption component where certain groups and people at the top, such as: ž

- **High-Level Administrators and Executives**
- **Financial Institutions**
- **Loan Servicers**
- **Stakeholders**

benefit financially from the current structure of the education system, at a significant cost to students (Debt burden, limited access, stress, and anxiety)

So while the student loan debt crisis in the United States is a significant burden for millions of students, many college campuses and their administrators continue to accumulate significant amounts of wealth, benefiting from tax exemptions and other financial incentives. You need to be aware of this component of corruption. This is a huge conflict of interest and the main reason of these flaws.

According to US Today, as of the first quarter of 2023, student loan debt in the U.S. stands at a total of over $1.77 trillion dollars. You would think this problem requires immediate attention and urgency but the influence of these special interest groups in the government is a barrier to reforming the higher education system who benefit from maintaining the Status Quo.

Unfortunately, these groups often have the resources and influence to navigate the system to their advantage. You don't think about this but this matters to you if you want to go to college, because a lot of the cost you are going to be paying it is because of this component. Due to these economic pressures where the success of an institution is measured by enrollment numbers and graduation rates. Universities have shifted their focus towards operating as degree-granting institutions rather than as places of deep learning and helping people live the life they want to live. The time spent in college, under this model, becomes a race to obtain credentials rather than an opportunity for students to immerse themselves in a transformative educational experience. This is not education. For many people, when they hear the word "education", they subconsciously associate this with a piece of paper that says that you completed a university course. That is NOT what education is.

What Education Should be

Education, in the broadest sense, is the process through which we acquire knowledge, develop skills, and cultivate reasoning and judgment. It involves the acquisition, refinement, and application of knowledge. Education should assist you in enhancing your capacity to perceive objective reality. Is about learning how to think critically and independently, fostering an inquisitive mind, and developing the ability to question, reason, and understand how the world works so you can navigate through it effectively.

As you see, education is not only the process of learning a specific profession. Getting educated goes beyond the traditional classroom or the pages of a textbook. It is a continuous journey of discovery, where the learning process is not confined to merely absorbing and memorizing facts. It is about understanding relevant information about the world and equipping yourself with the tools to make informed decisions, solve problems, and contribute meaningfully to society.

I am going to provide you with a list of different aspects of what education should do to your life. You should understand education and its core and what it really is to use it to your advantage to navigate life's complexities and understand how the world works to better serve yourself and those around you.

Education should…

Enrich Your Knowledge: Education provides a foundation of knowledge across various fields. This knowledge helps you understand the world better, its history, its systems, and the interconnections among different aspects of life. You should use it to your advantage, become an expert in your field and understand the dynamics of the industries and environments you operate in.

Develop Critical Thinking Skills: Education should enhance your critical thinking and teach yourself to analyze, question, and evaluate information. This skill is crucial for making informed decisions, solving problems, and navigating the complexities of life.

Enhance You Personally and Professionally: Education should help you discover your interests and talents, develop your character, and build confidence. Professionally, it equips people with the skills and qualifications needed to pursue their career goals and succeed in their chosen fields.

Preparing for the Future: This world is changing rapidly. Every year is different from the previous one when back 100 years ago every decade was not that different from the previous one. If you want to have a life of abundance, you need to stay up to date with technological advancements, changing job markets, and emerging global trends. If you don't you will stay average. Educate yourself to stay up to date in your field.

As you see education is not about only pursuing academic qualifications. A true education instills a love for learning that lasts a lifetime. It encourages curiosity and an eagerness to continue expanding your horizons, long after formal education ends. The end of academic education is not the end of your education journey.

> **Education is a lifelong journey of learning, personal growth, and the systematic pursuit of understanding, aimed at enhancing your individual potential.**

Cheap Blue Collar Careers That Make Good Money:

Just like we covered earlier in the book, not everyone is cut out to be an entrepreneur, some people do indeed prefer to work for a company or are passionate about a specific career, and that's totally fine and normal, we all find different things that work for us.

I want to talk about different types of jobs where there are affordable, short-term courses that you can finish just in a few months and you can make a very good income: *Blue Color Jobs.*

Blue-collar jobs are types of work involving manual labor or skilled trades. They are the types of skilled work that often involve physical effort or hands-on work.

Here are a few examples:

- Electrician
- Plumber
- Construction Worker
- Mechanic
- Welder
- Machinist
- Carpenter
- Painter
- Truck Driver
- HVAC Technician
- Factory Worker
- Landscaper
- Bricklayer
- Boilermaker
- Railway Conductor
- Fisherman
- Ironworker
- Crane Operator
- Heavy Equipment Operator
- Pipefitter

These jobs form the backbone of many critical industries and are essential to the functioning of both the economy and everyday life. You should take pride of taking a career like this, they are the ones who keep the country going.

Despite their importance, there's a common misconception that blue-collar jobs are less prestigious or lucrative compared to white-collar jobs, which generally involve office work or higher degrees of formal education. This stereotype is increasingly being debunked. Many blue-collar roles offer competitive salaries, electricians and plumbers can earn an average annual salary of $50,000 to $70,000, often with the potential to earn more as they gain experience. Mechanics and welders usually earn between $40,000 and $60,000 per year, especially in skilled trades where there is high demand but a shortage of qualified workers. Skilled electricians or plumbers can earn high wages, often exceeding those of some office-based roles.

As of April 2023, the U.S. Bureau of Labor Statistics (BLS) provided valuable insights into the demand and shortage of blue-collar jobs in the United States. Here are some key points based on that data:

There will be demand for the following jobs:

- Linemen and Electrical Power-Line Installer
- HVAC Technicians\
- Plumbers, Pipefitters, and Steamfitters
- Construction Workers and Laborers
- Welders, Cutters, Solderers, and Brazers
- Automotive Service Technicians and Mechanics
- Truck Drivers
- Construction Industry
- Manufacturing Sector
- Transportation and Logistics
- Utility Workers
- Healthcare Support
- Skilled Trades Shortage

The cost and duration of these certification programs for blue-collar jobs can vary depending on the field. But I can say this for certain. They are definitely cheaper than most college degrees and at the same time, you can make more money.

Expected income and time frames: The figures I will present below will vary based on factors like location, experience, and the employer. But it will give you a good overview:

- Electricians: Typically earn between $45,000 and $90,000 per year, with master electricians potentially earning more. Basic certification programs can take several months, but full apprenticeships for advanced qualifications typically last 4 to 5 years.

- Plumbers: Annual salaries range from $40,000 to $80,000, with experienced plumbers in high-demand areas earning toward the higher end. Initial training and certification can be completed within 6 months to a year, with advanced apprenticeships taking longer.

- Construction Workers: General construction laborers can earn between $35,000 and $60,000, while specialized roles like construction managers can earn upwards of $90,000. Some basic certifications can be obtained in a few months.

- Mechanics: Auto mechanics and diesel mechanics often earn between $35,000 and $70,000 annually. Basic certification programs can range from a few months to a year.

- Welders: Depending on skill level and specialization, welders can earn from $40,000 to $70,000 per year. Entry-level welding certifications can be completed in as little as 6-8 weeks, with advanced certifications requiring additional time.

- Machinists: The annual salary for machinists usually falls between $30,000 and $65,000. Certificate programs can be completed in about a year. Basic certification programs can range from a few months to a year.

- Carpenters: Carpenters' earnings range from $30,000 to $70,000 per year, with specialized or experienced carpenters potentially earning more. Short courses for basic skills can be completed in a few months, though comprehensive apprenticeships take longer.

- Painters: Professional painters can expect to make between $25,000 and $55,000 annually. Basic training programs can last a few months.

- Truck Drivers: Salaries vary widely based on the type of trucking, but generally range from $35,000 to

$80,000 per year. CDL training programs typically take about 3-6 weeks.

- HVAC Technicians: These technicians typically earn between $35,000 and $75,000 per year. Basic certification can be achieved in 6 months to a year.

- Factory Workers: Depending on the industry and role, factory workers can earn between $25,000 and $60,000 annually. Depends on the specific role, but many basic certifications can be completed in under six months.

- Landscapers: Annual earnings usually range from $25,000 to $55,000. Basic certification courses can range from a few weeks to several months.

- Bricklayers: Typically earn between $30,000 and $70,000 per year. Short-term courses for initial skills can be completed in a few months, with longer apprenticeships for advanced training.

- Boilermakers: Salaries for boilermakers range from $40,000 to $80,000 per year. Basic certifications can be obtained in a few months, with apprenticeships for higher qualifications taking several years.

- Railway Conductors: On average, earn between $40,000 and $85,000 annually. Training programs can vary but typically last several months.

- Fishermen: The income for commercial fishermen can vary greatly but usually ranges from $25,000 to $70,000 per year. Specific licenses and short-term training courses can be completed relatively quickly.

- Ironworkers: Typically earn between $35,000 and $80,000 per year. Basic training courses can be completed in a few months, with more comprehensive apprenticeships lasting longer.

- Crane Operators: Can earn from $35,000 to over $80,000 per year, depending on experience and location. Basic operator certification courses can range from a few weeks to several months.

- Heavy Equipment Operators: Usually earn between $30,000 and $70,000 per year. Certificate programs typically range from a few weeks to several months.

- Pipefitters: Salaries range from $35,000 to $75,000 annually. Initial training programs can be completed within a year, with longer apprenticeships for advanced skills.

I hope you find this information useful and gives you a better idea of what is out there and what is possible for you. There is a shortage in the majority of these fields, so you can easily find a job after you complete the certification program. If you are not attracted to entrepreneurship and owning a business, blue-collar careers present a viable and often overlooked path to financial stability.

I know that entrepreneurship and white-collar jobs are glorified by today's society, but blue-collar professions are equally deserving of the same respect and can be incredibly fulfilling since they play a crucial role in our society, keeping our infrastructure running, our homes functional, and our industries thriving.

The Trap of Pointless Degrees: Avoid These <u>At All Cost</u>

What if I tell you that a high number of college graduates don't end up using their degrees? I am going to give you the most underemployed college degrees that you should avoid at all cost. If you are wondering what "Underemployment means". I means scenarios where individuals with specific degrees, skills, or extensive experience end up in positions that don't require such qualifications, in other words people with degrees working jobs that don't require degrees. There is a lot of careers that will make you fall into this trap.

If you're considering the college route, it's crucial to take into account:

- The projected income you can expect
- The job market demand for your chosen field
- The cost of the career
- The long-term viability and adaptability of the career

- The demand for your chosen career in your specific location (or where you plan to live)

According to the Grand Canyon University about 81% percent of Americans go to college just based on the passion and love for the subject while only 19% percent of people choose their careers based on the guaranteed income they can expect.

This is a problem because you can end up with a worthless degree that does not help you make an income, leave you with a lot of college debt, and a job that has nothing to do with what you studied for. This is not a position you want to be in. Having passion is important, but economic viability is even more crucial.

So I am going to provide you the unemployment rate of recent college graduates in the United States as of February 2023 by major, according to Statista

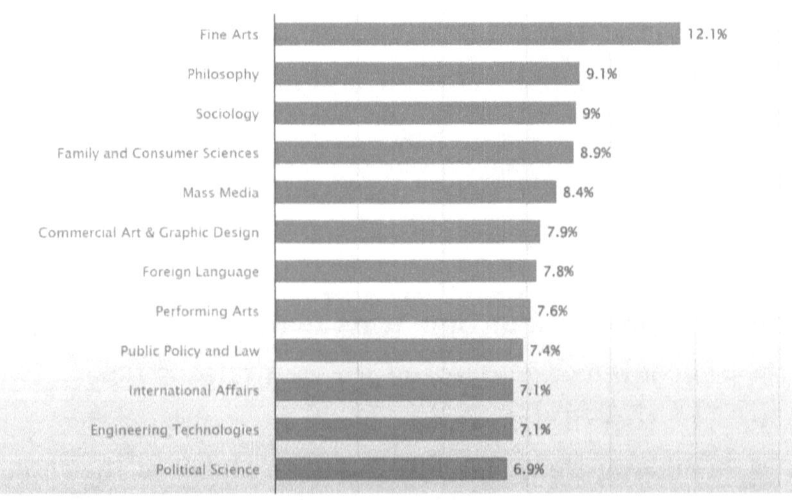

Every one of these is higher than than the unemployment rate in the United States at that time. Meaning that all of those majors the unemployment rate is above average. Graduates in these fields will face difficulty finding employment related to their degrees than graduates from fields with lower unemployment rates. Meaning there is less demand for jobs like this, also these skills are not easily transferable to other industries.

We do need to recognize that there are many degrees that are essentially worthless, with no demand or very little demand. Even if graduates can find a job with such degrees, they often don't pay well enough. When compared with the debt incurred to obtain the degree, it is still not worth it. If the degree cannot justify the expense and manage student loan debt, DO NOT PURSUE IT.

CHAPTER 5

Avoid Common Mistakes And Build a Fulfilling Life

We Are Living in the Best Times: The Golden Age for Opportunity

Not to give you a history lesson, but I want you to understand how fortunate you are to be born in this era. Despite the challenges and issues we still need to address as a society, if you look at the world from both a historical and global perspective, we have never been as prosperous, peaceful, and fair as we are today. This doesn't mean that there are no problems; issues such as income inequality, corruption, and many of the issues I discussed in Chapter 1. However, it is true that, on a global scale, we are doing a lot better in many ways.

For the vast majority of human history, a significant proportion of the world's population lived in conditions that would be classified as extreme poverty by today's standards. This state of affairs persisted until the Industrial Revolution in the late 18th and early 19th centuries, which marked the beginning of significant economic changes and improvements in living standards for many parts of the world. Before this period, technological advancements and productivity improvements were relatively slow, and economic growth was minimal or non-existent for long periods. Most people lived in agrarian societies, they relied heavily on farming, with little access to education, healthcare, and other services that contribute to a higher standard of living. Life expectancy was also much lower than today's standards, largely due to poor nutrition, lack of clean water, and limited medical knowledge.

I am going to tell you something that may shock you:

> **In numerous aspects of daily life and overall well-being, the average person today enjoys conveniences, technologies, and services that surpass what was available to even the wealthiest individuals in the past.**

It is crazy to think that even the wealthy in the past did not have access to many of the conveniences and advancements that are considered basic or standard today such as:

- Air Travel
- Internet and Digital Communication
- Personal Smartphones and Computers
- Modern Healthcare
- Automobiles and Public Transportation
- Electricity and Indoor Plumbing
- Air Conditioning and Central Heating

And many more…

This discrepancy highlights not just the technological and medical progress humanity has made but also the improvements in infrastructure, public health, and overall quality of life that have become more widely available over time. This transformation is a result of centuries of technological innovation, economic development, and social progress.

For most of history, the vast majority of people were peasants, laborers, or involved in subsistence farming. These individuals had very limited access to food, clean water, healthcare, and education. For the majority of the population, daily life was consumed by the struggle to survive. Long hours of hard labor with very little leisure time made life not only physically demanding but also monotonous. The lack of varied entertainment or the means to travel and explore meant that life could be dull and repetitive. Their living conditions often included small poorly constructed homes that lacked basic amenities like heating, plumbing, and ventilation.

Let me show you a typical house that people lived in throughout most of history:

For a large part of human history people lived in houses like this. Overcrowding was common, contributing to health issues. This is how the inside of that home could look like

Typically, these houses would have a single room that served multiple purposes: living area, sleeping quarters, and kitchen. The floors were often dirt or sometimes covered with straw to help insulate the room and provide some level of cleanliness. They could get quite muddy or dusty depending on the weather.

So we are doing a lot better in all the following areas:

- Extreme Poverty
- Life Expectancy
- Healthcare
- Hygiene and Sanitation

- Education access
- Technological advancements
- Quality of living
- Nutrition and Food Supply
- War frequency

Let's break these down a bit more...

Fewer in Extreme Poverty and Easier to Get Out:

- Global extreme poverty rates have significantly declined, and at the same time, escaping poverty is much easier now.
- Peace is at an all-time high, with fewer global conflicts and lower casualty rates, despite potential threats from modern weaponry.
- Medical advancements have led to effective treatments for previously fatal diseases, enhancing healthcare.
- Living standards have risen, thanks to improved housing, sanitation, and access to utilities, coupled with a rise in global income.
- Food quality has improved due to agricultural innovations and better distribution, offering a wider variety of nutritious options.
- Increased life expectancy results from better nutrition, healthcare, and public health efforts, leading to healthier, longer lives.

People get bombarded all the time with negativity in the news and the media. If you ask most people if the world is getting better or worse, the majority will tell you that it is getting worse when it is just not the case. If you think income inequality is bad now, it was a lot worse back then. If you were not born into a wealthy family, you were going to be either a peasant, serf, or laborer for the rest of your life.

When reflecting on this, I want to clarify again that I am not trying to deny the problems that we still have in society. As I mentioned at the beginning of this book, there are huge levels of income inequality and other problems that still need our attention. My intention in highlighting the progress we've made over time is not to deny these problems but to offer a counterbalance to the overwhelming negativity we get bombarded by from the mainstream media, which influences our perception of the world. If you are aware of this, you can cultivate a better understanding of the times we live in and encourage yourself to have a more positive outlook on the world, counteracting constant negativity. This will help you use the tools and knowledge to tackle the challenges that lie ahead.

There is opportunity Everywhere:

Since humanity has never been more equipped with the tools for health, prosperity, and knowledge. There are more opportunities at our disposal now than ever before; we have the power to shape our destinies, pursue our passions, and effect change not only in our lives but in the world around us, easier than ever before. The internet is only 25 years old and it has already sparked a monumental shift, setting the stage for an ongoing transformation with infinite possibilities.

The saying *"there is opportunity everywhere"* has never been truer than it is today. If you are able to have an open mind, a learner's attitude, and the courage to take that initiative, the paths to creating wealth, building careers, and achieving dreams are as diverse and plentiful as ever. There are so many opportunities out there waiting to be discovered by you, and you only need to milk one or 2 of them to make your dreams a reality.

You may be wondering how you can make this happen for yourself. Where do I start? Well I am going to provide you with a three-step process for going from where you are right now to seizing an opportunity and being in a desired position to a reality.

Step 1: Seeking the Opportunity

This step is about research and exploration, where you are actively on the search for potential opportunities and the act of discovery. Here is when you are going to utilize the tools at your disposal, research industries, trends, and the career paths you desire. Use platforms like YouTube, which offers countless tutorials on virtually any subject. There are knowledge gaps you need to cover and for this research is fundamental.

Step 2: Seeing the Opportunity

If you are looking for something, sooner or later, you are going to find it. You need to be able to identify when an opportunity is good for you. Makes sense for who you are, your current situation and your long term goals.
Step 3: Seizing the Opportunity

Now is time to prepare to engage with these opportunities actively. How? By contacting people., making yourself visible. Networking is crucial to infiltrating your desired circles.This final step is about taking decisive action—making the move to capture the opportunities you've identified and for which you've prepared.
Many times, you get what you dare to ask.

The act of asking can be incredibly powerful. You are opening doors for yourself. You can get information, and connections, and get yourself into situations that might not have happened if you did not ask. Whether it's for knowledge, help, or opportunities, the act of asking is a key that can unlock untold potential and lead to paths previously unimagined.

It's a simple concept: If you do ask, you have the possibility of a yes, either now or in the future; if you don't ask, the answer will always be no. You're not giving the opportunity even the chance to materialize.

Our lives depend so much on what we know and what we do. The more we know and the more we do, the better our lives will be, but the less we know and the less we do, the worse our lives will be.

The Future of Work and Money: Trends to Watch

Is your job safe? What will the world look like by 2030

Work is beginning to look very different across all fields around the world. Many experts argue that we are currently experiencing what some people call "The Fourth Industrial Revolution." This term came from Klaus Schwab, the founder of the World Economic Forum.

Just like in the past when we had the rise of agriculture and later the rise of corporations, which were driven by advancements such as steam power, electricity, and computing. Now, we are seeing the rise of technologies, such as artificial intelligence, the Internet of Things (IoT), robotics, blockchain, and other digital innovations that are changing every single aspect of our lives, across industries and society at large.

At the same time, we're witnessing the rise of the knowledge work era, where knowledge is becoming more important than labor. In this era, the ability to work with information, think critically, and innovate is becoming more valuable than manual labor skills. Which is what used to be valuable for most of history.

I could write an entire book detailing how this will unfold and how to prepare yourself for what's coming. But I am going to keep it short and to the point. I will offer you several insights and trends to watch over the next decade. Much will change, and you'll need to be adaptable because if you don't you'll stay behind.

Skills that will be in high demand:

- Digital Literacy & Computational Thinking: More and more skills will be needed to navigate digital technologies
- Critical Thinking & Problem-Solving: Vital as automation replaces routine tasks, you will require evaluation and complex problem-solving skills.
- Data Literacy: The world will become more digital over time. Knowing, interpreting, and analyzing data will be crucial.
- AI and Machine Learning Knowledge: Increasingly essential across sectors, even for non-technical roles.
- Cybersecurity & Information Security: As AI evolves, companies will need to protect themselves against evolving digital threats.
- Technology Integration & Automation: Important for improving efficiency and implementing new technologies.

- Interdisciplinary Knowledge: Means combining insights and methods from different subject areas or disciplines to solve problems.

Considering where we find ourselves and the direction in which the global workforce is heading, here are **six predictions of how the future of work will look like:**

1) Majority of people will be Freelancing: The standard 9-5 will is in decline. By 2035, the majority of the U.S. workforce will engage in freelance, contract, or gig work, driven by the desire for flexibility, autonomy, and the proliferation of digital platforms.

2) AI Fluency Will Be Required: Since AI will become the norm. Most workplaces are going to require some form of basic proficiency with AI and automation tools, regardless of their field.

3) Most routine jobs will disappear: By 2035, routine-based roles in sectors like manufacturing, clerical work, and basic customer service, will significantly decline due to automation and AI. By 2050 most of these jobs will be extinct

4) Increased Demand for Cybersecurity Experts: Since digital transformation is going on across all sectors, cybersecurity will become a critical concern. This will lead to a surge in demand for professionals skilled in protecting digital infrastructure.

5) Remote Work Becomes Standard: By 2030-2035, remote work or the option for hybrid models will become a standard offering across most industries, challenging traditional office-centric work cultures.

6) Emergence of New Job Roles: A whole bunch of new professions will emerge in response to technological advancements. As technology continues to evolve, the demand for professionals who can bridge the gap between innovative technologies and practical applications will grow.

What type of jobs are going to be created? Just to give a few

- Renewable Energy Technicians: Rising demand for solar, wind, and other renewable energy skills due to global green energy initiatives.
- AI and Machine Learning Specialists: Needed for the development and maintenance of advancing AI and machine learning systems.
- Data Privacy Officers: Essential for protecting data and ensuring compliance with privacy regulations amid increasing breaches.
- Remote Work Facilitators: Crucial for enhancing productivity and efficiency in growing remote work settings.
- Urban Farmers and Vertical Farming Specialists: Required for innovative farming methods like vertical farming to improve food sustainability.

- Cybersecurity Analysts: Increasing need for experts to combat sophisticated cyber threats and protect digital assets.
- Healthcare Navigators: In demand for assisting patients in navigating complex healthcare systems and making informed choices.
- E-waste Management Experts: Important for environmentally friendly disposal and management of increasing electronic waste.

You will be in the workforce one way or another in 2030 and beyond. You have to consider the future landscape of employment, especially if you're currently in roles that are heavily routine-based, such as manufacturing, clerical work, and basic customer service. These positions are going to be fading away year after year. While there will be a reduction in demand for certain jobs, simultaneously it will be an increase in demand for other jobs in areas related to these new technologies. So if you are in any of these sections where your job will be replaced in the future, you have to start thinking about reskilling or upskilling—acquiring new skills that are in demand and can safeguard your employability in the future. If you focus on skills that are less likely to be automated, you can secure your future.

Many resources are available to help with this transition, including online courses, vocational training programs, and professional workshops that can equip you with the skills needed for a successful career pivot. Embracing lifelong learning and being proactive about personal and professional development are key to navigating the changing employment landscape. While the shift can be challenging, it also presents an opportunity to explore new interests, develop new skills, and potentially find a fulfilling career path that aligns with the future of work.

Passion and Progress: Loving the Journey

If you find the way to have fun on your way to financial independence, you are in a position to have a great life.

I am going to teach you in this section how to change the perspective of viewing wealth creation and achieving the good life as a daunting task to a more playful approach where you can actually have fun with it.

Now here is the problem, if you don't like your life, it is going to be hard for you to adopt this mindset. You have to improve your environment since being in a comfortable and positive state is crucial for embracing this perspective.

I came out with 5 important points for this. Each point contributes to creating an overall life experience that is conducive to growth and satisfaction. Let's delve a bit deeper into each one:

Liking your job, or at least not hating it: You need to have at least some sort of job satisfaction. It is going to be very hard to be positive in your day-to-day if you hate your job. You may not have passion and love for it but at least you don't hate it, it pays the bills, and allows you to have income coming in, while you work on something else. If your current job isn't providing these, it may be time to consider changing to another job where you can have greater satisfaction, whether it's a new role, a different company, or even a career change. You want to be comfortable with your work, this will help you view the world more positively, and be more comfortable with your day-to-day life.

Be comfortable in your home: Your living environment plays another crucial role in your overall quality of life. You need to live in a place where you feel comfortable, safe, and relaxed. This environment will positively affect your productivity. Make sure that your place is nice and clean and you like it, combined with having a job that you don't hate will make things easier on you.

Hate your city or Neighborhood? You may consider moving: I know, easier said than done. But if you live in a city you hate, whether because it is a small town and there is nothing to do, or for whatever reason you have not been feeling it for a while, you want to consider relocating to a city that aligns with your lifestyle preferences or being close to nature if that's what you enjoy. The right location can offer access to activities you love, a culture you connect with, and opportunities that align with your personal and professional goals.

Making a decent income:
You need to either do two things. Make more, or spend less. Or both. You cannot be always short on money because you

are going to struggle and always be stressed. You need to find yourself more comfortable with your financial situation. You want to enjoy life's pleasures, but always have purchasing power for your needs and wants.

Passion for Your Side Hustle: If you have a side hustle, not only you want to understand it, but also you want to find some passion for it. A side hustle should be more than just a means to make extra money; it should be a source of fulfillment and an opportunity to pursue something you're passionate about and you are eager to see it grow. You are aware this may take years but you enjoy the journey. Seeing it grow it is a pleasure for you.

The journey to any goal is where life happens

There is a universal desire for us humans to achieve and reach various destinations, it is a fundamental aspect of life. From the President of the United States to an individual seeking personal wealth, everyone wants something. People regardless of their status and wealth have goals, aspirations, and a vision for what they want to accomplish. An essential part of this pursuit, often overlooked, is learning to appreciate and fall in love with the journey itself. For instance, a president may think he has accomplished a lot by being president in the first place, but is that the end of it? No. He has goals for his term in office. Similarly, a person striving for wealth will find that true richness comes from the experiences, relationships, and personal growth they encountered along the way. Wealth, in its broadest sense, includes not just financial abundance but also a wealth of experiences, knowledge, and emotional well-being.

So to recap, the path to financial independence and achieving life fulfillment is more enjoyable when:

- You enjoy your work
- You live comfortably in your home
- You live in a city that suits you
- You can secure a good income
- You have enthusiasm for your side venture

If you are in this position, consider yourself very fortunate. The path to any achievement is as important as the achievement itself. You are not where you want to be, yet still, you have a great life.

Self-awareness and having the least basic comprehension skills about how the world works will help you with this, Keep a few points in mind:

- You have to celebrate small wins: If you achieve something, feel good about it. it means you are getting somewhere, that you are in track and your work is paying off. Each small win is a step in the right direction since the path to success is a series of small steps, so each one deserves recognition. Celebrate your own way, the bigger the milestone the bigger the celebration.

- The Beginning is ALWAYS the Hardest

Nothing will be easy from the beginning. The more we do something the easier it gets, and this applies to anything new you start doing. The more uncertainty there is the bigger the difficulty will be, the same the other way around the bigger the familiarity and practice the better you will be at it. Every master was once a disaster.

- At the end of the day. It's All About Progress:

You first have to worry that you are moving forward, that's the the essence, regardless of the pace. Once you are there you can worry about speed. Learn to measure success by the progress made, not the speed at which milestones are reached. As you gain more knowledge and experience, you will find opportunities to accelerate your journey. Do not look for shortcuts, look for roadmaps. As long as you are moving forward, you are on the right path. Redefining your pace can come later; what's imperative is NOT to stand still.

Research/Action: Informed Steps Forward:

There is a time for research and there is a time for action. As information enters in, practical steps (action) should be going out. The less certain you are of something the more time you should take on research, it is ok to take action and learn on the way by doing because you need a foundation on what you are doing. Have your action predicated on informed research.

When ***uncertainty is high***, it often indicates that there are many unknowns. It's prudent to prioritize research over action. You should be gathering information, understanding risks, exploring alternatives, and taking the time to understand your next steps.

When uncertainty is low, it implies that you have a solid understanding of the situation, and the outcomes are somewhat predictable. This is the ideal scenario for taking action. With the foundation of strong research and clear insights, you can proceed with confidence, knowing that the likelihood of success is higher. In this context, action should indeed be high, as it capitalizes on the clarity and knowledge acquired through research.

So…

- If uncertainty is high ⬆ action should be low ⬇
- When uncertainty is low ⬇, action should be high ⬆

Now this doesn't mean overanalyze everything and fall into what we like to call "Analysis Paralysis" which occurs when an individual or organization spends so much time gathering information, evaluating options, and forecasting outcomes that they become unable to make a decision and take action. Don't let this be you, if you already know what you are working on and you spent the last few months or even year researching and not doing anything, there is time for you to recognize and stop this.

Redefining "Failure": It Is Feedback

Society's view of failure is wrong. It is portrayed as a negative endpoint, and and done deal. It is not. (Most of the time)

The word failure is used too often and depicts a final verdict on one's abilities and that discourages further attempts. In reality, with almost everything in life, the process of achieving something involves doing, failing, learning, re-trying, improving, rethinking, and building upon it. Especially when you are doing something for the first time, stepping stones, mess-ups and mistakes are normal and essential for getting ahead of anything. However, society often misconstrues failure as a definitive endpoint where you are done, rather than an integral part of the journey towards mastery and success.

This perception is erroneous, first, it ignores the reality of what it takes to achieve things, and second and more importantly it leads to a reluctance to try new things, it makes you give up too soon, making success not happen, not because you fail, but because you quit. This perception is deeply ingrained in cultural narratives, educational systems, and even in the professional world, where failure is often stigmatized. The perception of failure, then, becomes a self-fulfilling prophecy. If viewed through a lens of defeat, it can halt progress and stifle ambition.

Think about very successful figures such as Jeff Bezos, Elon Musk, and Thomas Edison to give you a few examples:

Jeff Bezos, the founder of Amazon, faced numerous setbacks and skepticism as he transformed a simple online bookstore into one of the world's most influential tech giants. It took him years until he was able to get Amazon to get track.

Elon Musk's ambitious ventures, such as SpaceX, encountered early failures with rocket launches that could have deterred a less resilient spirit. The first 5 attempts blew up. Yet, these failures were critical learning moments that paved the way for groundbreaking achievements in space exploration.

Thomas Edison was famous for how many times he failed before he was able to make it happen. Edison himself reframed these not as failures but as steps towards success, famously stating***, "I have not failed. I've just found 10,000 ways that did not work."***

These narratives underscore the essence of failure as not the opposite of success but a part of its process.So I want you to know that it is common, normal, and expected when you are doing something to find setbacks, to be stuck, to not know what to do, to feel lost, or to take it even further, to move on.

Even when you move on from something is because you either found that the endeavor you were on was not for you and to explore another path that often leads you to the same or even a superior goal. The reality is that most people fail at their first businesses and later find success with another business or venture.

> **_Failure is not the antithesis of success but a vital component of it. When you find an obstacle you are not supposed to surrender you are supposed to persist and beat it._**

If you understand and more importantly internalize the true nature of failure, which is an integral and inevitable part of the journey toward success, you will reap profound benefits since this will alter your approach to challenges and setbacks. This self-awareness is empowering; it instills resilience that encourages persistence rather than surrender when faced with obstacles. You need to understand that obstacles will come. There is no escaping them.

You should ALWAYS be anticipating and accepting this. It is a natural part of the process. This anticipation prepares you to navigate challenges with agility, viewing each setback not as a deterrent but as an opportunity for learning.

I mentioned it before and I will mention it again. DO NOT BUY into the hype that social media always shows you the glamorous lifestyle of people living the life, without showing you what it took to get there. You are only seeing the top of the iceberg. **Success IS NOT instant and effortless.** Recognizing this you will be ahead of the curve because most young people today are not aware of this and they will truly fail who you will persevere.

CONCLUSION:

I hope you enjoyed reading this book and found it valuable, I enjoyed writing it since I am passionate about understanding the dynamics of the world's elites and at the same time I love the journey of building wealth and having a good life. I hope you were able to learn a lot and use this information to better your own life and with that those around you.

If before reading this book you were in a position of being lost and oblivious of how the world works and after reading it to have a more clear direction on what you want to do with your life, I have achieved my goal.

Finding success and achieving the good life (Health, wealth, love, and happiness) is possible and easier than at any other point in history, despite the problems we still have as a society. The money will likely still flow up, and world governments will still do what is best for the elite of their countries and their donors, but at least you are prepared to take matters into your own hands.

We are always in the pursuit of something better, we are always attempting to improve, to get to the next level, to do something more meaningful and fulfilling. That's the very essence of being human. Like we discussed earlier our progress is tied to two main pillars: What we know and what we do. What we do with the knowledge we have, how we apply it in our daily lives, and the decisions we make as a result, ultimately determine our path and our progress. I hope this book has been a crucial tool in your arsenal, providing you with the clarity and understanding required to navigate the complexities of the world and to grasp what it takes to attain your aspirations.

If you have any comments or something that you would like to say about this book feel free to write me an email at contact@michaelwoodslife.com. I respond to every email I get. Any feedback you may have or something you think I should have included in the book or you would like to hear in the future.

If you took the time to read this book is because you want something better for yourself, you want to find wealth and have a life of abundance. I applaud you for that, you will find your way. I hope this book made it clear that the world is not how it is being presented, that there are multiple paths to achieve the same goal and that failure is not how we thought it was. Show up, do your best, and call it a day. You will see that just a bit of progress and work every day towards your goal will make you get there eventually.

Stay Strong
Michael Woods